What business leaders say about
Tim Stevenson and *BETTER*

"At last, a leadership book that is focused on behavior! As a pioneer in executive coaching, I know that leaders must understand themselves and address their behavior. Tim Stevenson has written a much-needed book for leaders who want to get **BETTER**. I have known Tim for a decade. He has been a leader for as long as I can remember, and it shows. As a coach, he is process-focused, authentic, and dedicated to his clients. As an author, he is both clear and compassionate. He brings you this book from knowledge, experience, and practice. Highly recommended."

— Brenda Corbett, Author & Co-founder
Sherpa Executive Coaching

"Leadership isn't *a* difference-maker. It is *the* difference maker. In short, leadership is influence based on trust you have earned. Through his fundamental leadership coaching, Tim has earned the trust of countless individuals. Tim's leadership insights are practical and full of wisdom."

— Daryl R. Flood, President & CEO
Daryl Flood Relocation & Logistics, Agent for Mayflower Transit

"I am very impressed with *BETTER*. It targets all the aspects of being a leader and how to maintain the position. Having spent a long career in the corporate world, I was amazed to find how comprehensive Tim's presentation is, addressing a number of subjects that are often not even on executives' radar screens. *BETTER* presents clear insights on subjects important for any leader, from the front-line manager to the CEO, and explains how to apply the principles to everyday work and life."

— R. J. Richards, National Director of Engineering (retired)

"Tim Stevenson is a prolific and intelligent writer, and this book proves it. In *BETTER*, Tim combines his many years of experience as a leader and developer of leaders with perspective gained through eight years as a university-certified Sherpa Coach. He is an expert on the topic of leadership, across industries and organizational charts. *BETTER* is a 'must-read' for leaders and for the coaches who make them better."

Karl Corbett, Managing Partner, Sherpa Coaching
Publisher, The Executive Coaching Survey

"Having worked with Tim twice in the past eight years, I continue to be amazed at how applicable his coaching has been throughout. The basic principles he introduces have been instrumental in my ability to navigate through many difficult situations, and his insight into human behavior has helped me understand what motivates others and drives my own behaviors. Tim's ability to apply these principles in actual examples easily synthesizes the message for anyone, regardless of their position or years of experience as a manager or leader. His clear, concise, yet thoughtful style facilitates both individual coaching and large groups. In short, Tim drills down to the root of who and what you are, then gives you applicable tools to use as you lead others to where they need to go."

— Katherine Johnston, Chief Administrative Officer
Southwest Pulmonary Associates

"I am fortunate to have had the privilege to know and learn from Tim Stevenson. As an executive leadership coach, Tim challenges his clients to reflect on, refine, and develop their leadership skills. *BETTER: The Fundamentals of Leadership* is sure to take you on a journey of leadership self-discovery and growth. I also appreciate Tim's *Leading Insights* articles, which offer practical, relevant solutions to today's leadership challenges written in a style that is brief, engaging, and informative."

— Laura Carr, Chief Operating Officer
Medical Practice Management Company

"After years of studying science and pursuing personal development, Tim Stevenson threw open the doors to new learning and challenges in the arena of professional leadership for me. His methods, presentation, and personal style make for a rich and exciting adventure down a clearly laid-out path, leading to accelerated professional and personal growth. Time spent reading *BETTER* will prove to be a wise investment in your leadership skill set and future success."

— Megan Conoley, M.D., Internal Medicine & Pediatrics
USMD Health System

"Tim has a rare gift of helping a person realize what their true gifts are and how to utilize them to achieve their goals. Tim and I have had a business relationship and personal friendship for over twenty years, and I consider him one of the wisest men I have known. He will help anyone reach their highest potential as a business person and a human being."

— Will Cureton, Partner
Ascension Development

"Over the years, I have read dozens of leadership books and taken part in several leadership development programs. While I make it a point to always take something away from these investments, Tim's coaching went past the typical teaching of 'principles' and gave me insight into some of my behaviors. This better understanding helped me become a stronger leader. Tim's coaching is practical and full of application. I would highly recommend him to anyone seeking to become a better leader."

— *J. Kelly O'Connor, Senior Vice President*
Daryl Flood Relocation & Logistics, Agent for Mayflower Transit

"Tim Stevenson has always displayed a calm, positive, and influential Leadership style with great proficiency in the Eight Key Management Competencies. He is known to be a 'People Developer' and does so in a caring and grounded manner. It is interesting … when Tim speaks, people listen, and it is not because he is the most outspoken person in the room. It is his wisdom that speaks volumes."

— *Peter McCampbell, President*
Human Capital Metrics

"Tim has the unique ability to break down complex ideas and problems and provide solid, easy-to-understand solutions — so easy to understand that you will think, 'Why didn't I see this before?' I've known Tim for more than 30 years, and I've benefitted greatly from him as a mentor and friend. He is a gifted communicator, teacher, and coach. If you want real help, let Tim come alongside you and help you see the clear path ahead."

— *Bob Christopher*
Author, Simple Gospel, Simply Grace

"Tim's insights into leadership and his engaging coaching style allowed me to discover my true leadership potential. Through his coaching, I was able to enhance my strengths and find opportunities to grow as a leader in my organization."

— *Stephanie Copeland, M.D., Chief Quality Officer*
USMD Health System

"*My favorite thing is to help people.*' This is what Tim said in 2013 when he announced he was leaving the company in which we both worked to pursue his vision independently. He changed my life, and not only helped me become a leader, but also a better person. How many times has someone lifted you from doubt and negativity and taught you to believe in yourself, given you confidence and faith in your own future? To coach and to have such a profound impact on individuals, you need more than knowledge; you need heart."

— *Joanna Diehl, Manager (a major airline)*

"Tim Stevenson has the ability to turn a problem into an opportunity and, further, to communicate to others how to do the same. It's a rare gift, and I have been the personal beneficiary of his wisdom, insight, and generosity of spirit. I'm so grateful!"

— *Steven Smith, Vice President*
Southwestern Baptist Theological Seminary

"Working with Tim over the last several years, learning and applying the fundamentals and disciplines found in the pages of this book, I've seen it work. Nothing can cripple an organization quite like a leadership void. Nothing can strengthen and accelerate a team's potential quite like quality, effective leadership. Study the principles in BETTER and you will find a common language and methodology for identifying and developing the leader within you and your organization."

— *Steve Weatherford, Vice President*
Daryl Flood Relocation & Logistics, Agent for Mayflower Transit

"As an executive coach, Tim helped me realize what my values are as a leader and what I want from members of my team. I was transitioning to a new executive role at the time, and Tim's coaching and methods helped prepare me to be a better executive and leader on day one. I use Tim's methods and recommendations to this day."

— *Robert Slaughter, Director of Clinical Services*
Cone Health Medical Group

BETTER

The Fundamentals of Leadership

What you must know and do if you
want others to follow you

Tim Stevenson

Stevenson Leadership Coaching

First Printing: May 2016
Stevenson Leadership Coaching
www.StevensonCoaching.com

ISBN: 0692707182

Table of Contents

Foreword

It has been almost 10 years since I met Tim Stevenson, and I remember it well. I was a 38 year-old Chief Operating Officer of a large medical group and was not enthusiastic about the prospect of spending the next 12 of my Tuesday nights for an hour or so after work to meet with the "mandated" executive coach for our C-level management team. I was doing just fine, given my ascension to the C-level suite at my age, and clearly needed no coaching in my mind.

But then I met Tim.

Tim changed my entire concept and understanding of leadership. During our time together, he not only showed me the vision of the leader I wanted to be, but the path of change I needed to forge to be the leader I now aspired to become. He took me on a journey of self-discovery and self-awareness, which made me nervous and uncomfortable, yet gave me confidence and a passion to improve. His style and teachings were powerful and insightful, but at the same time clear, concise, and easily consumed. I was hooked after our first coaching session, and today as the leader of a large Accountable Care Organization, I again turned to Tim to help develop all the managers on my team, and I regularly seek his advice and value his friendship.

I am excited for you to get to know Tim and his lifetime of lessons on leadership through this book. Whether you are a new manager or a leader for many years, I have no doubt **BETTER** will serve as an indispensable tool on your own leadership journey.

Steve Neorr
Chief Administrative Officer, Triad HealthCare Network
Greensboro, North Carolina

Acknowledgements

The importance of a leader's support network is emphasized in this book. I have been blessed with wonderful people in my life whom I wish to thank for their contributions to me.

My wife Suzanne: Loving, nurturing, protecting, a wise advisor, and ever-serving. Thank you for patiently enduring the writing of another book.

Our seven children and their spouses, six grandchildren (and counting), and our extended family. What blessings, and how thankful we are for all of you! I want especially to thank my uncle, Hoss Foncannon, who has demonstrated throughout his long life that an effective leader can also be a great guy and a lot of fun to be around.

My buddies and brothers, the V-Team. Twenty-plus years of Bible study, friendship, working, doing life together, and good beer. Luther and Melanchthon would totally get it. Thanks to Mike Messerli, Lionel Garcia, and Steve Weatherford for reading the manuscript and offering suggestions.

Brenda Corbett, Judy Coleman, and Karl Corbett, founders of Sherpa Executive Coaching, and my fellow Sherpas around the world. The decision to pursue a Sherpa Coaching certification was one of the best of my life. I sincerely appreciate you and your support. Thanks to Sherpa Brian McConnell for offering helpful suggestions.

Melissa Cox of ACLARUS Marketing and Steve Gamel of Edit This for their professional assistance, and my friends in the North Texas Business Network - owners of quality small businesses, and quality individuals.

Finally, I want to thank the hundreds of executive coaching clients and leadership training participants I've worked with. I have been inspired by your sincere desire and effort to stretch and grow in order to help make teams, organizations, and the world **BETTER**. It has been my honor and privilege to play a part in helping you achieve your goals.

Tim Stevenson
Flower Mound, Texas, May 2016

Introduction
The Challenge of Leading

Every significant group accomplishment — and failure — in the history of the world can be traced back to leadership.

Leaders make things happen. Ideally, leaders make things **BETTER**, though we have to acknowledge that many times they don't. Leaders have frequently led people, organizations, and whole nations to disaster. If you are one of those who wants to make things **BETTER**, I am writing for you.

I work chiefly with leaders of companies and nonprofit organizations, but the principles presented in this book can apply to anyone, whether your ambitions are for a small sphere like an office, classroom, or family or on a grand scale like a huge corporation, national government, or entire society.

The amazing and perhaps surprising fact is that *the fundamentals of leadership are the same, regardless of the size of the goal.* If you learn and practice the fundamentals of leadership, you are as equipped as you can be (in the present) to make a difference toward your desired target. I qualify that statement with "in the present" because there is no substitute for growing in experience and wisdom. That's Leadership Lesson One: *No one "masters" leadership.* For the best of men and women, leadership remains a lifelong pursuit, a continuing education and challenge.

My aim in this book is to lay out clearly what you must **know** and **do** if you want people to follow you. There are some natural questions I'd like to address up front.

Why another book on leadership?

That's a fair question. Today a Google search asking for "books on leadership" returned 407,000,000 hits. Is there really a need for number 407,000,001?

I have been a leader and an avid student of leadership throughout my life. I have read many dozens of books on the subject, not to mention thousands of articles. I've listened to hundreds of talks on leadership and have sought out the best authorities I could find.

I've benefitted from all those sources, but here's my observation: These books and resources tend to provide helpful insights and practical applications about leadership, some quite sophisticated. What they do not do, in my experience, is lay out the basics, the fundamentals of leadership. They do not systematically present the ABCs of leadership, those things must be known and applied by everyone from beginner to advanced practitioner. There is too much assumed, too much not addressed at all.

My desire is to help equip you with a foundation of leadership basics you need to know and apply in order to lead successfully and upon which you can grow as a leader for a lifetime.

Why me? Who am I to write a book on leadership?

Another fair question. I'm not famous. I've never led a Fortune 500 company or a branch of the military, nor have I held an elected office.

Here's what I have done. I have been an effective leader for more than 30 years, serving four organizations in the for-profit and nonprofit world. In 2007, I decided to specialize in this field, and I added certifications in Sherpa Executive Coaching and Sherpa Leadership Institute processes to my experience. In 2014, I was honored with the distinction of Master Sherpa Coach, one of only seven in the world as of this writing. My full-time emphasis today is helping men and women become more successful through becoming better leaders and growing in personal effectiveness.

Beyond being a successful leader myself, in every organization I've served I have created leadership-development processes. I have actively developed hundreds of other leaders, many of whom have themselves become leadership developers in countries all over the world. The principles we will examine in these pages are the same truths you would encounter if you were to attend my classes. The former clients and associates whose comments can be found in the opening pages are witnesses to my track record.

Former major leaguer and long-time broadcaster Johnny Pesky said this about baseball: "It's such a simple game ... and so very difficult to play." The same can be said about leadership. The principles we'll explore are indeed simple to understand, but be warned: They are deceptively simple! In reality, there's nothing more profound than fundamentals. Simple to grasp, yes, but a lifelong challenge to apply.

Why this heavy emphasis on fundamentals?

Every discipline has its fundamental principles. Some basics of financial management are the balance sheet, income statement, cash flow statement, and accounting principles. Engineers and physicists apply the mathematical basics: algebra, trigonometry, and calculus. In sports, you find recognized fundamentals for how to hit a golf ball or tennis ball successfully.

As a fuller example, let's consider music. The fundamentals include scales, chords, harmonies, and rhythm. A child picking out *Twinkle, Twinkle, Little Star* is applying them in simple form, but she is learning the very same principles that Bach, Mozart, and Beethoven used to compose the world's greatest music (in my opinion, at least). Naturally, the greatest composers add many layers of complexity, creativity, and brilliance, but they are building upon the same principles the child is taught.

This principle holds true even for jazz. Jazz musicians may appear to be breaking musical rules, but they are actually following a deeper understanding of the rules, which enables the creation of spontaneous freedom. Each member of the band knows and follows a common understanding of song structure, rhythm, chords, and scales, enabling them to make music together.

As we move ahead, we'll discover that successful leaders do the same. They may make it look easy and spontaneous, but the best leaders know and consciously apply leadership fundamentals. If they weren't, if they were truly violating basic principles, they would not be successful over time.

Fundamentals are the foundation for everything else

No one is perfect, meaning we all make mistakes. The best leaders do. Many mistakes can be overcome, but errors involving fundamental principles can take you out of the game altogether.

One of my favorite illustrations involves John Wooden, arguably the most successful sports coach of all time. Over a twelve-year period as coach of men's basketball at UCLA, his teams won 10 national championships, including 7 in a row. Wooden was and is widely revered by his former players and others as a great teacher of life, and his influence goes on through books and videos.

I heard a former player describe his very first practice under Wooden. A high school All-American, he arrived wide-eyed and eager to hear the words of genius and strategic brilliance of this world-famous coach. Wooden walked out to his team seated on bleachers and began quietly:

All right, gentlemen, the first thing we are going to do is to learn how to put on our socks and shoes correctly. You put your socks on like so ...

The player was shocked. "*This* is the genius of the great John Wooden?" He looked around to see how his teammates were reacting. All the veteran players acted like nothing was at all odd. They simply put on their socks and shoes just as Coach Wooden instructed them.

Telling the story years later, the player eventually realized that it made perfect sense. Your feet are your foundation as a basketball player. If you don't put on your socks and shoes properly, you could develop serious blisters, or perhaps turn an ankle. If you do, it won't matter how fast you can run or how high you can jump or how accurate is your shot. If you have blisters on your feet or a sprained ankle, *you won't be playing at all*. Your feet are your foundation.

I often think of this story when I meet people who turn up their noses at the thought of leadership fundamentals. Many foolishly seem to think they're "beyond" the basics, but in truth, you never are. No matter how smart, socially gifted, or attractive a man or woman is, if they violate the fundamentals of leadership, they will fall short, if not ultimately fail, as a leader.

So together, we will learn how to put on our leadership "socks and shoes." Then we will explore the applications of leadership in real life and prepare to play the game successfully.

Who you'll meet

This book is not a dry academic presentation of concepts. Points are illustrated by stories of real people struggling, learning, succeeding, and sometimes failing to become better leaders. Because confidentiality is a given in my coaching relationships, names and other identifying descriptions are changed, but every story is a true one. In the few cases where I needed to share more specific details, I have obtained permission from those clients to use their stories.

Most involve people I've coached or trained. Some are individuals I have worked alongside or observed. Many provide inspiring examples of humility, teachability, and sincere effort. A few exemplify an ironic proverb: "There's no such thing as a useless life; you can always serve as a bad example."

Some of the stories deal with people starting at the very beginning and growing as leaders. Others are about people encountering leadership challenges in the midst of their careers. All expose real-life hurdles leaders can expect to face and human-nature issues common to men and women. You can benefit from the experiences, good and bad, of others on the same challenging journey.

What you'll learn

Leadership is such a vast and complex subject that it would require a library to cover the subject adequately. The real-life demands of leading challenge you with countless unforeseeable situations and needs. That's why leadership is more art than science, making a knowledge of the fundamentals even more important.

The key to leadership is the leader. You are the focus of this book: What you must *know* and *do* if you want others to follow you. God willing, this is the beginning of a series of books to address important leadership applications. Here I am attempting to lay down essential first principles.

This book is divided into three parts:

Part I consists of three chapters, which form the foundation for our investigation, beginning with the elementary question, "What is a leader?" We will also address whether or not a particular personality or temperament is necessary and learn what is required to win followers.

Part II presents the requirements of effective leadership in my **10 Leadership Propositions**. These are 10 assertions that are essential to know and practice for successful, long-term leadership. They form part of the cost you should count before pursuing a leadership role and the awareness you need for your leadership journey.

In **Part III,** I share insights and essential equipment from a coach's perspective for moving ahead in leadership and some helpful tools. To apply these tools, you can download a free Leadership Self-Assessment I have created for my clients from my website, www.StevensonCoaching.com.

Each chapter in the book is followed by a summary of takeaways called "Leading Insights" (also the title of my free e-newsletter) to help crystalize and capture its major applications.

My life is dedicated to serving people and helping them be more successful, both professionally and personally. Leaders have the ability to make this world a **BETTER** place. I can't think of anything that would fulfill me more than having people read this book and go out to do exactly that.

May you richly succeed as one of them!

BETTER

The Fundamentals of Leadership

Part One

Your Leadership

Foundation

Chapter 1
This Is a Leader

There is a famous story about Vince Lombardi and the Green Bay Packers when they were enjoying one of most successful dynasties in pro football history in the 1960s.

Uncharacteristically, the team had played poorly over a stretch of games, and Lombardi grew increasingly angry. Finally he blew. At the team meeting following a loss, he shouted his assessment of their recent play in colorful terms. He concluded his tirade with, "I will not stand for it! We are going back to the very beginning! We're going back to basics!" Lombardi paused, holding up an object.

"Gentlemen," he said, "*this* is a football!"

A cheerful voice interrupted from the back of the room. It was veteran wide receiver and "class clown" Max McGee. "Hey, slow down, Coach," he called, "I'm taking notes!" The mood was broken by laughter, but they did get back to basics and got turned around.

People often need that kind of simplicity to understand leadership. What is a leader anyway? How can you know if you are one or could be one with study and effort? More to the point: Do you have what it takes to be a leader? You might be one of those who confidently says, "YES!" Or you might be among the many more who respond, "I think so," "I'm not sure," or even, "I doubt it." However you answer, my reply to you is "Not so fast!" We first need to establish how we are going to answer the question.

Related to that question is this: How can you know if someone else is a leader?

There are countless misconceptions, misunderstandings, and outright wrong answers you'll hear thrown about. If you don't have a clear definition of what a leader is, it's not possible to answer those questions accurately.

What does a leader look like?

What does a leader look like? "I know one when I see one," is a common answer. Not necessarily. How do you know a leader when you see one? What are their characteristics?

People usually say the same predictable things. They describe leaders as strong, charismatic, magnetic, attractive, energetic, courageous, and bold. They get it done. They're visionaries. They're impressive. They inspire and direct others with confidence.

I call this the Conventional Model. Someone who is extraverted and has a pleasing appearance, physically and verbally. They are confident in social situations and tend to stand out in a group. In fact, when leaders are chosen based on criteria like these, they often turn out to be physically taller than average. They are assertive, verbally adept, and present their ideas and opinions confidently in a crowd. These are the ones people point out as a "natural born leader."

Do you see the implications if this is true? Quieter, introverted, less socially-confident people need not apply. In fact, if you are physically shorter than average, forget it.

As valuable as natural gifts may be, they don't equate to leadership. *Some of the greatest leaders in the history of the world did not fit the mold of the Conventional Model.* If you are fortunate to possess some of those natural positive qualities, that's great; just be sure you don't rely solely on them. You need to learn the leadership fundamentals like anyone else, or you'll be in continuous jeopardy.

Organizations make the same mistake

Executive and author Max De Pree observed, "Choosing leaders is the most vital and important matter corporations and institutions face."[1] What if they are being chosen by the wrong criteria?

Companies today invest many thousands of dollars in sophisticated 360 degree feedback, leadership style testing, and personality and temperament evaluations. As a coach, I appreciate data and make good use of it whenever it's available. However, in most cases, those expensive reports with all that data presented in impressive-looking binders sit on office shelves gathering dust. The average person doesn't know what to do with it.

Organizational failures are usually leadership failures, and one of their chief causes is wrong people in leadership to begin with. How did those "wrong people" get into those positions? The common scenario is that they were chosen based on their professional competence (knowledge and skills) without regard to their proven leadership ability. That's why it's almost a rule of thumb that failed executives were hired on the basis of their professional competence and fired because of their inability to manage the people side of their jobs.

What about when companies provide "leadership development training"? Despite much money and effort, many of these don't do any better in producing new and better leaders for their organizations. A major reason why is that they typically use the Conventional Model to pre-select candidates for their program.

These organizations' desire and effort are commendable, but there are several things wrong with their common philosophy and methods. To them I say:

1. By pre-selecting your leadership candidates, you are passing over who knows how many people who don't fit the Conventional Model, but who may have the greatest leadership potential in your organization. Typically, you won't even notice them.

2. What is commonly called "leadership development training" in most companies is actually a form of continuing education; mostly skills, tools, and techniques. They provide good and helpful material, but that's not really leadership development. Though I don't want to issue a blanket judgment, I've observed many people in "leadership development" roles in companies who have never actually led anything, nor have they truly developed any leaders. The fact that people with only academic credentials are filling so many of these roles is itself an indicator of the problem.

3. By that method, your actual record of developing new and better leaders will not be much better in the long run than if you had no method at all.

I want to assert the next points as boldly as I can:

4. **You *cannot know* what someone will become.** There are people who jump out at you early with their evident qualities, but they eventually fade out, shoot themselves in the foot, or crash in leadership situations. There are others who do not initially stand out in the crowd, but who are capable of becoming world-transforming leaders.

    One vivid example was Thad, who showed up for a training class at our nonprofit organization after enduring a family tragedy. Awkward and needy, he admitted he was starting at the beginning, but had arrived at a place in life where he strongly wanted to learn. As humble and teachable persons do, Thad learned quickly and applied what he was learning. A matter of months later, he was assisting others in learning more about family and life skills. Two years later, he was serving as my substitute teacher and eventually took over the training as the instructor. A few years later, he was a member of our nonprofit board and was actively helping hundreds of other people in need. No one would have picked out Thad from that early training class as a future leader, but that is precisely what he became.

    After more than three decades of developing leaders, my ability to predict whether people will develop into leaders is higher than it was in the beginning. Even so, I've learned the wisdom of reserving judgment. You can't tell just by looking, especially early in the game. It's wiser, for many reasons, to wait and see. And you must know what to look for!

5. **The idea that you can gauge someone's "leadership potential" early in the process is a myth.** Those who talk confidently about someone's "leadership potential" are almost always viewing them through the lens of the Conventional Model. If this is, as I suggest,

the wrong criteria, then it should come as no surprise that the results of those leadership development efforts are mediocre.

The myth of leadership potential

When I hear talk about someone's leadership potential, I am reminded of a story about a grizzled, experienced baseball manager. A reporter was enthusiastically extolling a young prospect's potential. He could run like Henderson, hit like Williams, throw like Clemente. His potential was unlimited! He was ready for the Big Leagues right now! Tell the Hall of Fame to reserve a spot!

The old manager shifted his chaw of tobacco from one cheek to the other, spit, and said, "Let me tell you something about potential." He paused and looked the reporter in the eye. "Potential will get you fired."

To that veteran manager, this was an old story. The history of baseball is littered with accounts of can't-miss prospects that failed to make a dent in the Major Leagues. Many managers have been fired in baseball because upper management decided "they weren't getting enough out of their players." Why did they think so? Because "there was so much potential in the club."

That manager also knew what many people in organizations have forgotten about leadership: **Performance is reality** — not potential, not appearances, not glibness or being socially smooth. To be direct:

(If you've forgotten your math symbols, $\neq$ means "does not equal.")

A pleasing personality	$\neq$	Leadership
Good looks	$\neq$	Leadership
Professional competence	$\neq$	Leadership
A strong work ethic	$\neq$	Leadership
Being verbally smooth	$\neq$	Leadership
Popularity	$\neq$	Leadership
A strong will	$\neq$	Leadership
The smartest person in the room	$\neq$	Leadership

What is the application of these observations to leadership? Simple. There is one, and only one, way to know if someone can be an effective leader.

The only way to know if someone can be an effective leader: You see him or her do it!

When you see someone successfully lead others, that's when you know he or she is a leader. Everything prior is sheer guesswork. This principle highlights the consequences of the common practice of elevating excellent individual contributors to leadership positions. Since you cannot know if someone has genuine leadership ability before actually seeing them win and lead followers, such a promotion is a roll of the dice. The results of this situation can be observed in the high percentage of executive failures in organizations.

That should be both sobering and encouraging. Sobering for those of high confidence, especially if you aren't sure why you're so confident. Understanding leadership should be sobering to anyone, in fact, because of the high demands, potential risks, and difficulty of the role. But the assertion above should also be *encouraging*. Whether you possess or lack the usual qualities associated with a "natural born leader," leadership is a subject that can be studied, learned, and improved with effort and persistence.

For the rest of this book, let's put away the whole nebulous phantom of "leadership potential" and your self-judgments on the matter. We'll concentrate instead on what leadership actually *is*, what you must *know* and *do* if you want people to follow you, and understanding the key concepts and applications necessary for leading successfully.

What is leadership?

What is leadership, anyway? According to the dictionary, leadership means "the ability to lead." That may not appear very helpful, but notice one thing: "To lead" is a verb. That indicates *action*.

You may think that any subject on which there are thousands of books would have a standard definition. Oddly, I don't think I've come across the same definition twice. Each book seems to present its own version. I have collected quotes on leadership for years. Many of them offer genuine attempts at a definition. Some make insightful observations. Some are cynical or tongue-in-cheek. Here are several (my comments follow in italics):

Warren Bennis "Leadership is the capacity to translate vision into reality."
Not bad, some truth in that, but how do you do it?

Napoleon "A leader is a dealer in hope."
That could be good if the hope is realistic and not a deception (note the source). Hope does accurately point to the fact that leaders deal in a better future.

Condoleezza Rice "Power is nothing unless you can turn it into influence."
Not directly about leadership, but it's pointing to it.

John Maxwell "Leadership is influence — nothing more, nothing less."
Maxwell's widely popular and he likes power statements like this, but it's not enough. A crook who pulls a gun and demands your wallet is certainly going to "influence" you, but I wouldn't call it leadership!

John M. Burns "Leadership is when persons with certain motives and purposes mobilize, in competition or conflict with others, institutional, political, psychological, and other resources so as to arouse, engage, and satisfy the motives of followers."
What? Way too wordy and obscure to be much help.

Vance Packard "Leadership is getting others to do something that you are convinced should be done."
That's true to a point, but there are many ways to get people to do what you want that have nothing to do with leadership. Too many managers don't get this. See above comment on Maxwell.

Bergen Evans   "For the most part our leaders are merely following out in front; they do but marshal us the way we are going."
Cynical definition, but it definitely reminds me of some career politicians I've observed.

John Naisbitt   "Leadership involves finding a parade and getting in front of it."
Another version of the cynical view.

Theodore Roosevelt   "People ask the difference between a leader and a boss. The leader leads, and the boss drives."
Insightful and true. I'll come back to this one later in the book.

Frances Hesselbein   "The leader beyond the millennium will not be the leader who has learned the lessons of how to do it ... The leader of today and for the future will be focused on how to be — how to develop quality, character, mind-set, values, principles, and courage."
Thoughtful comments from the woman management guru Peter Drucker called the most effective leader he knew in the world.

Alan Sugar   "Effective leadership is about earning respect, and it's also about personality and charisma."
I was OK with it until "charisma." If he's correct, I'm in trouble. It's also untrue. Many great leaders have been charisma-challenged.

Clarence Randall   "The leader must know, must know that he knows, and must be able to make it abundantly clear to those around him that he knows."
*Sounds good ... until as a leader you run into a situation and realize you **don't** know; in fact, **you have no earthly idea what to do.** Get ready: You can expect that to happen to you sooner or later as a leader. What then?*

There are many interesting points made in those quotations, but where do you end up? What is a leader and what is leadership?

It's time for my "this is a football" definition.

This is a leader

At the beginning of my career I heard a series of messages on leadership from Dr. Howard G. Hendricks (1924-2013). You may not have heard of the man affectionately known as "Prof" by his students at Dallas Theological Seminary, but he played a major role in developing more effective leaders than almost anyone in the world. I still have recordings of those messages and listen to them often.

In them (speaking to an all-male audience) Hendricks gave this definition: "A leader is a man who knows where he is going and is able to persuade others to go along with him." Obviously, for you ladies: "A leader is a woman who knows where she is going and is able to persuade others to go along with her."

From the time I heard that definition, it clicked with me. I have used it ever since, for myself, and for the many people I've trained and coached.

Let's test it. Think of the most successful leaders in world history. What names do you come up with that fit that definition of a leader: People who knew where they were going and were able to persuade others to go along with them? I've done this often with classes, writing the names they proposed on a whiteboard. Here is a representative sample of answers:

Jesus Christ	Winston Churchill
Gandhi	George Washington
Eleanor Roosevelt	Jackie Robinson
Vince Lombardi	Florence Nightingale
Teddy Roosevelt	Abraham Lincoln
Ronald Reagan	Martin Luther King
Henry Ford	Queen Elizabeth I
Mother Teresa	Frederick Douglass
Julius Caesar	General George Patton
Billy Graham	Rosa Parks

Predictably, as American groups their answers are skewed to the United States and Europe, but that's beside the point. Despite the fact that there is a wide variety of personalities, temperaments, and styles represented here, all of them *knew where they wanted to go and were able to persuade others to go along with them.*

That's not the end of the discussion, however. It isn't long, sooner or later, that someone adds to the list:

Adolf Hitler	Joseph Stalin
Osama bin Laden	Napoleon
Mao Zedong	Jim Jones
Genghis Khan	Saddam Hussein

Upon reflection, you'll quickly see that these nefarious characters were also "successful" in knowing where they wanted to go and in persuading many others to go along with them.

How useful is a definition of leadership that can take in, for example, both Mother Teresa and Adolf Hitler? After all, it doesn't address the leader's goals, message, methods, or accomplishment. It doesn't address ethics, morality, or integrity.

The irreducible definition

Let there be no misunderstanding about this. I am an unapologetic advocate for **principled, values-based leadership**. That means:

1. Leadership that is aimed at goals that are *honorable* and *good* for individuals, organizations, and society; not selfish hidden agendas or covertly self-centered

2. Leadership that is based on *honest mature communication*; not communication that is manipulative, deceptive, or childish

Even so, the definition above is useful. *This is the irreducible definition of a leader*, meaning leadership is much more than this, but it cannot be less. This is bedrock. An irreducible definition is necessary as a minimum starting point. I for one have no interest in helping people achieve evil or selfish ends or in becoming more effective at manipulating or using others. But knowing that some leaders have led others to bad places should serve as a warning to all of us that, like any form of power, leadership can be used for good or bad purposes. Just as the same hammer can be used to build a useful structure or to bash someone's head in, leadership is a power that can be used for honorable, admirable, and selfless purposes or dishonorable, evil, and selfish purposes.

Your primary leadership responsibility is not about what you want others to do. It is managing *yourself.* People are always asking, "What should I *do?*" That is not the most important question. *Being* precedes *doing.* Your initiative in self-management and self-development is always primary. You truly control only yourself.

It doesn't matter how brilliant, attractive, or persuasive leaders are. If they do not have authentic substance at the core, they will fail. That's why I apply an inside-out pattern to life and leadership. Wise leaders know the battle never ends. They do not become complacent, believing they "know enough" or are ever "good enough." They keep pushing the boundaries of their knowledge and skills and remain open to further learning and correction.

We have much to examine and learn. As we prepare to move ahead, here is the definition of leadership we will use and build upon for the remainder of this book.

How can you know if you are a leader?

You are a leader if you know where you are going and are able to persuade others to go along with you.

Impress that definition in your mind as we go to work in the next chapter.

Leading Insights

Part 1: Chapter 1
This Is a Leader

- Some of the greatest leaders in the history of the world did not fit the mold of the Conventional Model of a leader.

- The idea that you can gauge someone's "leadership potential" early in the process is a myth.

- The only way to know if someone can be an effective leader: You see him or her do it.

- Definition of a leader:
  You are a leader if you know where you are going and are able to persuade others to go along with you.

Chapter 2
The Common Denominators

You are a leader if you know where you are going and are able to persuade others to go along with you. Both halves of this definition are essential.

The first part answers the question, "What do you want?" It really doesn't matter how popular you are or how good you might be at getting an enthusiastic crowd together. If you don't have a direction or goals you want to pursue, the best you can create is a party ... or a riot. A well-known saying puts it, "If you don't know where you're going, then any road will take you there." Another says, "If you aim at nothing, you'll hit it every time." Unless you are prepared to answer the "What do you want?" question, you are not prepared to lead.

Though it is essential to know what you want, it is not sufficient. The second half of our definition of a leader says you must be able to persuade others to go along with you. If you can't, it won't matter how clear-cut your goals or how exciting your vision. You'll be going there alone. Without followers, you are not a leader.

Where are you going?

Leaders are trying to accomplish something, go somewhere, fix a problem, or achieve a vision. *They are future-oriented.* This doesn't mean you have to know all the answers by any means! If fact, some of the most important leadership examples in the world begin when *nobody* knows what to do, but some man or woman speaks up and says, "We have to do something about this. There must be a way to make this better. Let's go to work." They stimulate a process whereby a group or team puts their heads together and attacks a challenge.

Several years ago, I put a man named Larry in charge of an important committee on a major project. He seemed the ideal choice. Everybody loved

Larry. In fact, he's on a short list of the most popular people I've ever worked with. But he proved to be a poor choice as committee head on this occasion.

They started out well, but after a few weeks, I started hearing complaints. "All we do is talk endlessly," one person said. "We're not accomplishing anything," another related. In the beginning, these comments just seemed like a little background noise. I realized it was more when, a week later, a committee member came to me and told me directly, "You have to do something."

The first thing to do was to investigate, to ask questions and listen. After talking with Larry about how he thought things were going and then talking with members of his team, it became obvious what the disconnect was. The committee members were highly motivated about their task and eager to make decisions, take action, and get the job done. To Larry, however, the process itself was exciting and fun. He felt successful when his team actively participated in discussion, regardless of whether they actually did anything meaningful. He loved talking. He loved the exchange of creative ideas. He loved people. People also loved Larry, but they were ready to strangle him. He clearly needed some coaching on team leadership.

That's what I had to do. I started working with Larry on how to pursue greater accomplishment with his team. He needed help identifying concrete objectives, accomplishing goals, and being action-oriented. He was teachable enough to receive coaching and improved, and that committee went on to work much better together. I also learned something: People are not equal in their understanding of the role of a leader. I learned that what is obvious to me might not be obvious to someone else, and that I must set clear expectations and offer coaching and guidance when I commission a person or team to accomplish a task.

Mostly, Larry's story illustrates why popularity does not equal effective leadership. You must know where you want to go and possess the drive to press on in that direction.

Where are your followers?

The world is full of people who have noble ambitions, big ideas, and accurate assessments of problems. That alone doesn't translate to leadership. Many of these people can make a logical and emotional case for why others should get on board with their cause, but they're unsuccessful in winning followers. Why? Sometimes it's easily explainable. Sometimes, you can't put your finger on why someone can't gather followers. They just seem to be missing *something*, some undefined ingredient.

I worked alongside Jonah for many years. He was a good guy, dedicated, and very smart (a Ph. D., in fact). Many times he came up with ambitious plans for getting people together to work on projects. He wanted to create training classes to teach others, and was well-qualified when it came to knowledge. However, year after year I watched Jonah get minimal results from his efforts. For some reason, people weren't inspired to join up with his programs. They liked him all right, they just didn't want to follow him. There was no glaring weakness I could identify, no character flaws, no personality warts. He merely lacked some quality that attracted followers.

Jonah remained a valuable individual contributor, but he had little success as a leader.

Can anyone learn to lead?

Frequently people have asked me, "Can anyone learn to become a leader?" I answer this way: "*Most* people can learn and *improve* as a leader." I say "improve" because we must face the fact that we aren't created equal in terms of capabilities. World-class leaders are rare, and I would never say that just anybody can achieve that level by working hard. But most anyone with the desire can "improve" as a leader with diligent study and persistent effort.

But no, there are people who **cannot** learn to be a leader. Here are some:

- Those who lack sufficient **Emotional Intelligence**, also called **EQ** as opposed to IQ (intellectual intelligence or brain power)

To win followers you must have sufficient understanding of human nature and social situations. People with high EQ can pick up on subtle signals and social clues such as facial expressions, tone of voice, and body language. They can sense what others are feeling. Just as important, they can also anticipate the effect of their words and actions, allowing them to communicate strategically to win followers.

Warren was tall, good-looking, and likeable. In social settings, he did well. He seemed to have all the natural elements to be successful as a leader. Warren, however, had an unfortunate tendency to "drop bombs" on people and walk away oblivious to the effect he created. It was not that he said blatantly offensive things, but his attempts to communicate were somehow off-center or subtly negative. He seemed unable to predict the effects of his words or notice afterward that he had left people feeling "funny." Even though Warren was granted several platforms to perform in leadership, he never attained more than modest success. After watching for many years, I came to the conclusion that he lacked some aspect of EQ.

Emotional Intelligence is one of the areas in which we are not created equal. The important application for aspiring leaders is that there is a *floor*, a minimum amount of EQ a leader needs. People below that threshold will not be successful leaders. The good news is that it is possible for most people to improve in EQ with persistent learning, effort, and experience. A coach or mentor is often helpful to grow in this area.

- Those who **do not want** to become leaders

It might be surprising to learn that not everyone wants to be a leader, in the same way that not everyone wants to climb the corporate ladder. Sometimes it's a matter of personal priorities and values. Many people simply prefer to be followers of an effective leader.

Some don't want to be leaders because they rightly recognize that leadership is a burden. It means additional responsibilities. Leadership can make you a target, and many people aren't willing to risk that. They are following the advice offered by Harry S. Truman: "If you can't stand the heat, get out of the kitchen." They're happy to leave the heat to others.

- Those **unwilling to pay the price leadership requires**

These might be people who wish they were leaders, or who make resolutions to develop as leaders. Often they lust for a position, but are unwilling to bear the burdens of actually doing the position. It's one thing to "BE" the leader, another thing entirely to "DO" leader. Many want the *title*, *prestige*, or *recognition* that goes with a position of authority, but that's a far cry from bearing the daily responsibilities of leadership.

More is required of you if you are a leader. We'll discuss in my **10 Propositions** some of the specific additional burdens that go with leadership, and we'll see that there is a definite "counting of the cost" that you should do *before* pursuing the role. It will also be necessary to embrace the preparation and ongoing self-maintenance you need to succeed over the long haul.

This survey of people who cannot be leaders is not meant to discourage you, but to give you a realistic caution. More is required of you if you are a leader, so you need to go into it with your eyes open.

What about personality and temperament?

Successful leaders come in all shapes and sizes, all personality and temperament types. There is no single mold you must fit into in order to become an effective leader.

If I may use an analogy, I like to compare it to batting styles in baseball. I trust that even if you aren't a baseball fan, you know enough about the game to follow my points.

I've always been fascinated by the variety of batting styles players use. A batter's stance and practice swings are so individual that you can present silhouettes of famous hitters, and an avid baseball fan will identify the player. When I was young, my brothers and I used to play a game like that. We'd pick up a bat, take a stance and a few swings, and say, "Who's this?" We could almost always guess correctly. "Willie Mays." "Johnny Bench." "Ernie Banks." "Frank Robinson."

One of the earliest professional coaches to bring a scientific analysis to batting was Charlie Lau. In the 1970s, Lau became curious about how batters could appear so different, and yet, be successful. Rather than rely on decades of conventional baseball wisdom that had been handed down, Lau decided to use films, video, and photographs to examine the methods of the game's greatest hitters.

Lau looked at the best players of his time and also the great players of the past: Ruth, Cobb, Hornsby, Musial, Williams, and so on. He discovered that despite the wide differences in style, there were some things every one of them did. One of his observations that most arrested my attention as a young ballplayer was this: At the instant the pitcher releases the ball, *every successful hitter is in the exact same position.* His weight is on a firm back leg, his front foot is prepared for a forward weight shift, and he holds his bat in what Lau called "the launching position."

So after being fascinated for years with the variety of ballplayers' batting styles, I came to realize that they are actually irrelevant. It doesn't matter what weirdness or gymnastics a batter does to get ready. He must do exactly the same as every other hitter when the ball is released, or he won't be successful.

The same thing is true in leadership. It is not about the style, personality, or temperament of the leader, though all these play a part in their make-up and how they go about it. No matter how flamboyant or how unassuming a leader might be, those are not the things that determine his or her success.

Some of the historical leaders we'll consider could not be more different in personality, temperament, or style, but at the core of their leadership were common qualities. Every one of them exhibits the characteristics of the **10 Leadership Propositions** in **Part II**. And while there are differences in the preferences of various age groups (boomers vs. millennials, e.g.), they all respond to leaders who display the fundamentals of leadership.

The differences are superficial - the fundamentals are the same

Yes, we have to admit that when people are asked to describe what a leader looks like, they usually answer according to the Conventional Model:

extraverted, impressive, aggressive, and excellent orators. They can make a speech and get a crowd to storm the gates. Some of the historical persons mentioned in Chapter 1 do fit this category: Julius Caesar, General Patton, Vince Lombardi, and Teddy Roosevelt are classic examples.

Others fit the description of standing out in a crowd and attracting almost automatic responses from followers through their charisma. George Washington is consistently described by contemporaries as producing that effect. He often didn't have to say much of anything. Just his physical appearance, dignity, and demeanor aroused confidence, even in dire circumstances.

With some, it's not so much their charisma, but an uncanny way of delivering an inspiring message that induces confidence, courage, and commitment. Winston Churchill emerged after what he called his political "wilderness years" to galvanize Great Britain through his speeches to fight against almost impossible odds. Martin Luther King did the same in his battle for civil rights. Ronald Reagan was dismissed for years as an ex-movie-actor and advertising pitch-man, but his ability to connect through language with the American people made him a powerful leader for the USA and the free world.

Many famous leaders did not bloom until later in life. Eleanor Roosevelt, for example, struggled with feelings of inadequacy and rejection from childhood. Believing she was unattractive and undesirable, she lived quietly in the shadow of her husband Franklin D. Roosevelt for years. If Eleanor had worked for a modern corporation, no one would have gushed over her "leadership potential" or picked her for "leadership development training."

But in middle age and with the platform of being First Lady, Eleanor found increasing strength through her deep personal convictions and her ability to create a network of friends and likeminded men and women. She grew into a powerful advocate for the poor, women, and civil rights, expressing opinions decades ahead of her culture. The list of her accomplishments is truly amazing. Recognizing her influence, her husband's successor, Harry S. Truman, called Eleanor the "First Lady of the World."

Contrasting styles, similar success

If you compare leaders who share similar positions, you'll see wide contrasts in personality and style. George S. Patton was a fiery, over-the-top military commander, but compare him to General Omar Bradley. General George Marshall described Bradley as "quiet, unassuming, capable, with sound common sense." It was reported at the time that when he gave orders to soldiers of any rank, he usually said "Please." Good qualities, but not the first ones that come to mind when you think "great leader." Except that Bradley was the one chosen (over Patton, among others) to command the entire American ground forces invading Germany from the west after D-Day.

General Dwight D. Eisenhower, their superior and Supreme Commander of Allied Forces in Europe, was known for his friendliness and likeability. His most famous attribute was his confident grin. Though excellent at military strategy, his greatest leadership achievement may have been relational. To win the war in Europe, Ike had to get the highly competitive, jealous, egotistical, and sometimes self-centered military leaders of several Allied nations to work and fight together. It was the ultimate challenge in herding cats, and he pulled it off successfully.

In sports, compare Vince Lombardi with his rival, Tom Landry, head coach of the Dallas Cowboys for nearly 30 years. Lombardi was the prototype of the loud, emotional, inspirational football coach. "If you are not fired with enthusiasm," he shouted, "you will be fired with enthusiasm!" Lombardi's speeches and sayings continue to inspire people in all kinds of fields more than 40 years after his death.

Tom Landry couldn't have been farther apart on the temperament scale. He was cerebral, even-tempered, and unemotional. "Stoic" was often used to describe him. His intellectual, low-key style was criticized by some players, who said he was "remote," "distant," and "cold." Even so, many of those same critics look back on Landry today with admiration and gratitude. Years and maturity helped them understand Landry's character and the wisdom of his methods and appreciate his impact on their lives. Both of those men, as different as they were, rank among the most successful football coaches of the 20th century. Both modeled useful applications for effective leadership.

I've seen the same kinds of contrasting styles in people I've trained and coached over the years. Some fit the description of the charismatic natural leader with a commanding presence that inspires others to follow. Many of these possess strong, unbending wills to overcome obstacles and succeed. If there's something in their way, it's going to get moved. People quickly line up to follow them.

But I've seen just as many others who are quiet and introverted and not particularly assertive, especially about themselves. They are kind, compassionate, and considerate in their dealings with others. They genuinely care about the people they seek to lead, and their followers believe in them. Some of these have been just as *effective* in accomplishing goals and mobilizing others as their more fiery counterparts. They are successful in winning followers committed to their cause.

Proven by performance

This view of leadership temperaments has been demonstrated by research at the highest levels. In the bestselling book *Good to Great*, Jim Collins and his team investigated the characteristics of the best-performing companies. The finding that most surprised him and his fellow researchers involved what kind of leaders led those companies. Most people would expect to find the Conventional Model heavily represented: Larger-than-life, charismatic, celebrity-type executives at the top. Their research revealed *exactly the opposite*.

The best companies are led by what they call Level 5 Leaders. These are characterized by "a paradoxical blend of personal humility and professional will."[1] The reference to personal humility does not mean these leaders lack ego. On the contrary, they have strong egos, just as most leaders do. But the focus of their ego strength is the *success of the enterprise, not themselves*. That's where their "professional will" is directed.

Other terms they use to describe the various Level 5 leaders include humble, modest, self-effacing and workmanlike. Some are described as introverted, mild-mannered, or shy.

How many people on the street would name these as "leadership attributes"? I can't resist asking as well: How many people with these attributes would be picked for "leadership development training" in the average company? You know the answer: Not many. And yet, the real proof of performance demonstrates that men and women like these have led the best companies in the world. A decade later Collins led another research project. In the resulting book *Great by Choice*, their earlier conclusions on leadership were confirmed.

In the book *Collective Genius*, a recent investigation of the world's most innovative companies, coauthors Hill, Brandeau, Truelove, and Lineback make the same observation. They flatly state that leaders of innovative companies do not fit the popular conception of a good leader. Instead, they tend to be thinkers, idealistic, generous, and willing to admit their own weaknesses and imperfections and ask others for help. They are action-oriented and demanding, yes, but demanding in regard to accomplishing the objective and in harmony with those other qualities. It's another example of that paradoxical blend of personal humility and professional will identified by Collins.

The authors go on to pose a question without offering an answer: How will more leaders like those be found in a business world that doesn't recognize them as "leadership material"? That's my question exactly and why I'm making such a point of challenging the Conventional Model and the methods by which many organizations pick leaders.

One of my strongest convictions is this: **You don't "pick" leaders. You IDENTIFY them.** It's my hope in this book to stimulate whole organizations, as well as individuals, to look at leadership development through a new and truer lens and to learn how to identify and develop the leadership ability that's right before their eyes.

Are there some temperaments that find it more natural to be assertive? Yes, absolutely. Are there people with certain personality types who take to leadership more easily? Again, the answer is yes. Some people with less assertive natures might need the right kind of coaching and mentoring to begin discovering "the leader within," but they can. Sometimes, these less forceful individuals prove to be the best leaders when they are cultivated in the right kind of environment and allowed to spread their wings.

The bottom line for you: *You don't have to fit any particular mold in order to be an effective leader.* There is no "right" kind of personality or temperament. **You can be yourself,** *because a person of any temperament can grow into an effective leader.*

Yes, you can be yourself … but at a minimum, you must do three things, all of which can be seen in the examples of leaders we've considered. Two of them come directly from our definition of a leader. The middle point is the thing that connects them.

To be an effective leader, you must:

1. Know what you want
2. Be able to communicate clearly
3. Be able to win followers

In the next chapter, we will begin at the end by discussing how to become someone able to win followers.

Leading Insights

Part 1: Chapter 2
The Common Denominators

- Unless you are prepared to answer the "What do you want?" question, you are not prepared to lead.

- More is required of you if you are a leader. There is a definite "counting of the cost" that you should do before pursuing the role.

- Successful leaders come in all shapes and sizes, all personality and temperament types. There is no particular mold you must fit into.

- Differences between effective leaders are superficial. The fundamentals are the same.

- You don't "pick" leaders. You identify them.

- To be an effective leader, you must:
  1. Know what you want
  2. Be able to communicate clearly
  3. Be able to win followers

Chapter 3
Preparing to Lead

The *process* of leading begins with knowing where you want to go, but that is not where leadership really begins.

A championship basketball coach was asked about the famous phrase "will to win" and its role in his team's successes. The coach replied, "The most important thing is not the will to win. The most important thing is the will to prepare to win." He was saying that championships are won on the practice floor, in the weight room, and in chalk talks long before the games are played. A team that neglects that preparation and tries to succeed on the basis of their "will to win" in the games will come up short.

Interestingly, the same truth was taught by the ancient Chinese sage Sun Tzu in his classic *Art of War*, written more than 2,000 years ago. He wrote, "Victorious warriors win first and then go to war, while defeated warriors go to war first and then seek to win."

I want to assert the same thing about leadership: The most important thing is not your desire to lead, but your diligence in *preparing* to lead.

To be an effective leader you must, at a minimum, do three things:
1. Know what you want
2. Be able to communicate clearly
3. Be able to win followers

I said previously that we will begin at the end, with the ability to win followers. This is because your ability to win followers cannot be something you try to figure out at the moment you want to lead. If you wait until "you know where you are going" before you begin to ask yourself how you can "persuade others to go along with you," *it will be too late*. It must be part of your continuous preparation long *before* the moment of opportunity or need.

Authority is not the same as leadership

Why should people follow you? That really is the heart of the issue, isn't it? Immediately we are faced with the issue of authority. Someone is the boss, the manager, the officer. He or she has authority delegated from above that grants them power over people below.

Delegated authority is simply a part of organizational life. Authority is a good thing, but it also implies accountability and responsibility. The manager has power over his or her sphere, but they are also accountable to those above with responsibility for results. I am not questioning this reality, nor that it is a good thing when applied well. It provides the organization necessary for large groups of people to do anything in concert.

What I am asking a person with authority, though, is, "Why should people follow you?" It's a question about leadership.

Mediocre bosses answer, "Because I'm the one in charge. Do it, or I'll get someone else." They are relying on their authority to get obedience. Let's face it. Soldiers in the army don't have much choice if they are given orders by a superior officer. Neither do most employees in most companies. Since virtually all of us need to work in order to pay the bills, we have to do what we're told or risk losing our jobs.

To that boss I counter, "That is not leadership. The most you can get through authority alone is *compliance*. A leader can stimulate *willing commitment*."

When I ask managers why people work at work, many answer, "Because they get paid to do it."

I reply, "No, that's why they have a *job*. What I'm asking is why they care. Why do they apply effort? Why do they go above and beyond?" I assert that if they do these things on a regular basis, it's because of effective *leadership* on the part of their manager.

The same kind of confusion can be seen in other realms where people hold a position with significant authority. I was talking recently with the chief physician of a medical company, and he asked me about some of my past experiences. I mentioned that in my last full-time position I had created a leadership development process for the company's physicians.

"Aren't *all* physicians leaders?" he snapped back.

"*Nooo*," I laughed. "Physicians are good at *being in command*, but that's not the same thing as leadership." I went on to explain the difference. "Your training makes you good as the unquestioned authority commanding a team and giving orders; in an operating room, for example. Leadership is about influencing people to follow you willingly, including outside that sphere. You might be able to command obedience in the OR, but you need to be an effective leader to lead other physicians or a team in an organization. You can't just command them."

You may now or in the future hold a position with significant authority. That's good, you can do a lot of great things when equipped with authority, but only when it is empowered as well by effective leadership. I think that's what Condoleezza Rice meant by her comment, "Power is nothing unless you can turn it into influence." Raw power is not enough.

The question of character

Without calling attention to it, I have repeatedly used the term "*winning followers*" in these early chapters. That is deliberate. The question is how to stimulate people to *willingly* follow you as a leader.

Yes, there are extreme occasions where a leader must force people to follow. That might be appropriate in wartime or in an emergency, but it is certainly not to be considered normal. There have been many managers in companies who have only gotten people to do their jobs through holding an "organizational gun" to their heads. Reliance on threats and intimidation signifies a failure of leadership.

It also brings us to the common question, "Is character necessary for leadership?" My answer is, "It depends what kind of leadership is called for." Usually, the answer is yes. Proven honorable character is needed for long-term effective leadership. An exception, however, is *crisis* leadership. In a crisis, typically, all people want is results.

Randall was a physician, with whom circumstances forced me to associate for a long time. Being blunt, he was one of the most unpleasant, least-likable persons I've been around. I think most others felt the same. He is one of the few people I've known whom I would grade as having zero leadership ability.

However, imagine this scenario: Several of us are seated around a lunch table when someone in the restaurant collapses. Randall is the only physician around. Who should take the lead? Of course, Randall should. What you want in a time of crisis is expertise. No one at the moment is concerned with Randall's likability or character. The rest of us, myself included, can only be available to serve, including taking orders. If Randall tells me to do something, I'm going to do it as quickly as possible to help in this crisis.

The ailing person is helped, and we're all relieved. But what happens when the crisis is over? No one is prepared to anoint Randall the leader of the group now that things have returned to normal. He is just as personally unpleasant as before, and our opinions of him are unchanged.

The same kind of dynamic can be seen throughout history for whole communities, even nations. When the barbarians are at the gate, we don't care about someone's character; we just want someone with B.O. bad enough to scare our enemies and lead us to victory. That doesn't mean we want that warrior to reign over us in a time of peace.

Many a man or woman has stepped into a breach in a company or organization and taken decisive action to solve a problem. These people have often been granted leadership positions as a result, and proven to be failures. The reason? They did not understand or embrace the full-orbed requirements of ongoing effective leadership.

Jim Collins has stated this truth as well as anyone I know (emphasis his):

Leadership cannot be assigned or bestowed by power or structure; you are leader *if and only if people follow your leadership when they have the freedom not to.*[1]

That is why I refer to "winning" followers. So what does it take?

Measuring your real impact

If you ask reasonably successful persons, "Are you good at what you do?" I can predict what most of them will answer. It will be along the lines of, "Yes, I know my stuff, and I work hard."

There's a lot more to succeeding than knowing your stuff and working hard, however. In Sherpa Coaching, we use a concept called **Impact On Business**™ (**IOB** for short) to examine someone's *complete* effect in their organization, which I am sharing by permission. IOB is also a way of calculating your true value to your organization or team.

POSITIVE **SKILLS** + POSITIVE **BEHAVIOR**
Professional · Leadership
Technical · Motivation
Business · Communication
=
POSITIVE IMPACT ON BUSINESS

What is someone saying when they answer the question, "I know my stuff, and I work hard"? They are talking about *knowledge and skills*, along with effort. I lump these together into the category, **professional competence**. Professional competence is a very good thing. Some level of competence is necessary in order to succeed in any role, and that includes leading.

Under the heading of professional competence, you'll find things like subject expertise, business knowledge, education, technical knowledge, systems, processes, financial management, and more. These are all good characteristics, things useful to succeed in any kind of business. The question, however, is not whether or not these are good things. The question is whether they are *sufficient* in themselves to allow you to succeed as a leader.

Notice what that list under the heading of knowledge and skills does not include: *There is nothing on that side that addresses* **behavior**. This missing focus has been repeated countless times in organizations where it has been foolishly believed that behavior is irrelevant, that only professional competence leading to results matters.

Professional competence is not enough

An extreme example of the logical extension of this mindset can be seen in the 2014 film *Whiplash* [caution: for those sensitive to profanity, this movie is severe in that regard, with abusive F-bombs and other curses dropped by the minute]. The movie follows the journey of an ambitious young drummer named Andrew and his desire to play for a world-class jazz band at a prestigious music academy. The band is led by Terence Fletcher, played by J. K. Simmons, who won the Academy Award for Best Supporting Actor for his performance.

Though initially thrilled to have the chance to play for the internationally-renowned Fletcher, Andrew is horrified at the behavior he witnesses. Fletcher proves to be nothing less than a sadistic sociopath. The musicians are terrified of him. He manipulates, insults, and abuses the members of his band viciously and quickly turns on Andrew. As the story unfolds, it is revealed that a former student had committed suicide due to Fletcher's abuse. Fletcher may be a genius in jazz music, but he's a monster as a human being.

Though not as extreme, I've encountered "Fletchers" in real life. There are countless individuals in companies and organizations who believe that only knowledge and skills matter; that they can do what comes naturally in terms of how they behave.

Stu was a director, an acknowledged expert on the subject matter of his department. He was up to the moment on the latest technology, laws, and regulations. Unfortunately, he was also caustic, insulting, and negative in his view of most people. His critical tongue knew no bounds except in the presence of his superiors where Stu would turn on the charm. He abused his staff who endured him only for the paycheck. Employees, including those at the director level and above, would rather contract the flu than work with him voluntarily. And yet, Stu still considered himself leadership material. He was incredibly self-deceived.

Dr. Bill was a physician leader in his hospital. Superficially, he possessed the usual qualities associated with the Conventional Model. There was only one problem. Bill had a nasty temper that could blow with little warning. He would become insulting and abusive, berating and belittling employees for their "stupid mistakes" and rampage through his clinic. Like Stu, Bill considered himself a leader and casually overlooked his out-of-bounds behavior. Perhaps as a surgeon, he was used to giving orders and impulsively saying whatever he was thinking at the moment, but that doesn't work under normal circumstances with people. Bill was also self-deceived and didn't realize that people who worked around him dismissed him completely as a leader.

Foolish managerial logic

Occasionally you'll run into executives who freely acknowledge that they are jerks. Oddly, they take pride in it and actually credit being a jerk for their success. "I get results!" they proudly proclaim. Others declare, "I have to be a *&#@! I can't afford to be a nice guy! How could I get people to work or hold them accountable otherwise?"

Managers like this are falling for a classic logical error. In formal logic, it is called the *post hoc ergo propter hoc* fallacy (*post hoc* for short). The Latin translates, "After this, therefore because of this." The example often used to depict this fallacy is the rooster. He crows just before dawn, then the sun rises. The rooster begins to believe that his crowing *causes* the sun to rise. Foolish managers like the examples above reason, "I am a jerk, and I get results. Therefore, I get results *because* I'm a jerk."

I reply with these questions:

"So there are no nice executives and managers in the world who get good results?"

"So you are saying that if you actually treated people with courtesy and respect, you would not be able to lead them to work hard or hold them accountable?"

"So you believe that by treating people this way you are leading them to achieve all they are capable of doing individually and as a team?"

Simply by asking the questions, you can see how ridiculous such a mindset is. There are uncounted examples of executives and managers who are principled, respectful, and kind that have led organizations and teams to *world-class* achievement. I assert further that principled, respectful, and kind leaders are far more likely to develop high-performing teams. They create cultures in which people thrive and are self-motivated to pursue excellence.

No, executives who act like jerks are succeeding (if at all) *in spite* of their behavior, NOT *because* of it. Besides falling for the *post hoc* fallacy, managers like that display practically no understanding of human nature or what truly drives performance. They're blind as bats. They may get some results in the short run, but they demotivate and burn people out (examine their turnover record). They do not lead teams to sustainable excellent performance.

Beyond professional competence

If you want to win willing followers, you must face the other half of the IOB equation. Your real Impact On Business™ is determined by your professional competence AND your **personal conduct**. In other words knowledge and skills + ***behaviors***. What kind of behaviors? Things like leadership ability, personal example, attitude, living your values, communicating, delegating, listening, team facilitating, teamwork, cooperating, approachability, and many more. In the business world, these are often spoken of dismissively as "soft skills" as opposed to the "hard skills" listed under professional competence.

What if we add some more behaviors? Consider if these would make a difference in leading: Maturity, courtesy, respect, consideration, manners, kindness, resilience, resourcefulness, reliability, truthfulness, flexibility, patience, and perseverance.

People may call behaviors "soft skills," but make no mistake about it: No matter how technical or numbers-driven a business may be, business is about *people* working with *people* to get things done with and through *people*. The idea that you can neglect the people side of business and still be successful is as foolish an attitude as someone can get.

Many assume that the issues of behavior and building relationships apply less as someone rises in organizational power. In other words, as people climb the corporate ladder, how they behave or get along with other people becomes unimportant. *The exact opposite is true.* At the higher levels of leadership, behavior becomes *more and more* important.

In the first chapter, I mentioned that it is almost a rule of thumb that failed executives are hired on the basis of their professional competence and fired because they cannot successfully negotiate the people side of their jobs. This is confirmed by Daniel Goleman, famous for creating the concept of Emotional Intelligence (EQ). He says (emphasis mine),

> When it comes to leaders, effectiveness *in relationships* makes or breaks. Solo stars are often promoted to leadership positions and then flounder *for lack of people skills.*[2]

This idea should make perfect sense with a little thought. People at the upper layers of corporations are assumed to be intelligent, knowledgeable, and hard-working. They are assumed to be experts in their field. However, as they rise, they are less called upon to do the work so much as seeing that the work *gets done by others* and *in partnership* with other departments. That puts a premium on leadership and managing ability, their ability to build positive professional relationships and collaborate with other leaders — all traits found on the right side of the IOB equation: Personal conduct or behaviors.

Leadership and behaviors make the difference

Imagine the "Acme Widgets Company." In the building across the street is "Beta Widgets Incorporated," which is comparable to Acme in size and history. Acme is twice as profitable as Beta. What do you think is the real difference between them? Knowledge of the widget business? No, they've both been at it about the same number of years. Education of the executives? No, they have received roughly the same university and industry training. Intelligence? No, they are about the same. There aren't any spectacular geniuses at Acme, and the executives at Beta are not idiots. In the real world, in fact, no organization has executives that are *that much smarter* than their competitors'. So what makes the biggest difference in results?

Mark it down. The reason behind one organization's superior performance over another organization equivalent in expertise and resources will be its executives' leadership ability and behaviors. It will be found in their ability to build a healthy values- and performance-based culture by design and inspire people to give their best in cooperation with one other in pursuit of organizational effectiveness.

The subject of this book is leadership, so let me modify the IOB formula and make it more specific. Rather than Impact On Business™, we will refer to **Your Leadership Effect**. Since you now understand the concept of IOB, we can simplify the equation to this:

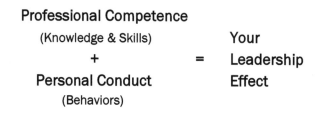

Your Leadership Effect means the total measure of your leadership influence over others. It will ultimately determine whether or not people choose to follow you.

Professional competence is still necessary

As we approach the end of **Part I**, I want to make sure there is no misunderstanding. Professional competence *is* one-half of your Impact On Business, and therefore one-half of your Leadership Effect. A sufficient measure of professional competence is *necessary* as part of your preparation for leading.

If you are perceived by others as lazy, sloppy, or incompetent at important work applications, it won't matter how likeable you are. You might be universally popular and even loved, but that does not translate to leadership ability. You must demonstrate a sufficient level of professional competence or no amount of good behavior can win followers.

Think of competence like the qualifying round of a professional golf tournament. Players must score in the top of the qualifying field just to make it into the real tournament to compete for prize money. The qualifying round represents competence, and prize money symbolizes leadership influence.

Therefore, if you aspire to lead, you must embrace from the beginning your responsibility to demonstrate competence in your area of work or contribution, along with a strong example of good habits, effort, and reliability. That will earn you the opportunity to earn leadership influence.

People are watching

What does this mean to you? It means people are watching. If you aspire to be a leader, you absolutely must embrace the truth that your behaviors are continually on display and will make or break your success at persuading others to follow you. Throughout the chapters ahead, we will spell out specifically what kind of behaviors to be aware of and practice.

It is critical to know why people follow or don't follow a leader. We'll find the answers in **Part II** of this book as we walk through my **10 Leadership Propositions.**

We are now ready to begin Part II with the number one reason people are willing to follow a leader, a quality so important that I call it *"the currency of leadership."*

Leading Insights

Part 1: Chapter 3
Preparing to Lead

- The most important thing is not your desire to lead, but your diligence in preparing to lead.

- The most you can get through authority alone is compliance. A leader can gain willing commitment.

- No organization has executives who are that much smarter than their competitors'. The explanation for superior performance will be found in its executives' leadership ability and behaviors.

- You must display a sufficient level of professional competence or no amount of good behavior can win followers.

- Your Leadership EFFECT (professional competence + personal conduct) represents the total measure of your leadership influence over others.

- Your behaviors are continually on display and will make or break your success at persuading others to follow you.

BETTER

The Fundamentals of Leadership

Part Two

10 Leadership

Propositions

Leadership Proposition 1:

The *Currency* of Leadership Is *Credibility*

Lawrence seemed to have everything you are looking for in a business leader. His professional competence was without question. He was intelligent, hard-working, and dedicated. He knew the business inside and out and was a major driver in the company's advances. Lawrence's character and values were also widely acknowledged. He was impeccably honest and sincere in his spiritual commitment to his faith.

There was only one problem. He grated on people, and some didn't want to work with him or under him.

Despite his unquestioned professional competence, Lawrence was stumbling as a leader. My job, when called in as executive coach, was to find out why. What was Lawrence doing or not doing that was undermining his ability to win followers?

Why people follow a leader

To understand why people do not choose to follow a would-be leader, we must first understand why they *will*. It really boils down to two reasons:

People will follow a leader ...
1. Because of their trust or confidence in the leader
2. Because they believe the future will be better if they do

It's really no more complicated than that. While the implications and applications of leadership multiply into the thousands, the reason people choose to follow a leader boils down to one or both of these two options. That is why these two motives provide the first of my **10 Leadership Propositions**.

Take the first point. People choose to follow a leader because they believe in her or because his ability and character are real and dependable or because she has a previous record of attainment or because he is what he appears to be, and that is an example of admirable qualities.

The second point, believing that following the leader will result in a better future, is also common sense. After all, no one will knowingly follow a leader to someplace worse. No one would follow a leader who openly said, "Come follow me, and you'll experience the humiliation of failure and the agony of defeat!" We have already acknowledged that leaders *have* frequently led groups, companies, and even whole nations to disaster. But the people who followed them believed the future would be better if they did. They just proved to be wrong.

No, we choose to follow because we think the future will be **BETTER**. This is where we speak of some leaders as "visionaries." They seem to have the ability to peer into the future and see a vision of an ideal world or situation and then persuade others to follow them into it.

The problem is not everyone has that ability to visualize the future or the goal. Even if the visionary's objective is valid, the average person may not be able see it clearly and perhaps not at all. That means the first reason, trust in the leader him- or herself, becomes the dominant motive in why people choose to follow.

The currency of leadership

If you think back to leaders you have followed, I bet you'll find this in your experience. There was something about them that inspired confidence. You believed they were honest, that they were what they seemed to be; that they were competent, they knew what they were talking about; that they had a future-oriented viewpoint, they were going somewhere good; and that there was something about them that inspired you, and you felt a little more (or maybe a lot more) positive about future possibilities.

How did they do it? Obviously, that's what this whole book is about. But the first thing to focus on is *the leader him- or herself.* The key words that pop up repeatedly are "trust," "belief," and "confidence." Describing that thing effective leaders have, we could use terms that might be clumsier, but they state the truth: Trustworthiness … Believability … Confidence-inspiring.

Or the word I choose that sums up this whole subject: CREDIBILITY.

Credibility is the currency of leadership. With sufficient credibility, you can successfully call people to follow you. If you have a great deal of credibility, you can even challenge people to do things that cost them time, effort, and comfort, perhaps even to the point of self-sacrifice.

Mother Teresa was a striking example of the power of impeccable credibility. This was a small woman who fit no one's picture of the Conventional Model of a leader, but she attained world-wide influence. I remember her on one occasion rebuking the President of the United States to his face in public without receiving a whimper of defense. He and others might later have said they simply "disagreed" with her opinion or that it was "more complicated" than she let on, but notice: No one **dared** to say a word against her personally. Decades of dedicated, loving, hands-on service to the most wretched poor, diseased, and dying in Calcutta earned her that credibility.

With sufficient credibility, you can win followers. With enough credibility, you can even call out a U.S. President. Without credibility, you can't persuade a puppy to go along with you.

Think back to a regular group you've been a part of, whether at work, school, or an area of personal interest. There is normally at least one person in a group that when he or she talks, people listen. Others look directly at them, stop what they're doing, and listen carefully. That is someone who has earned significant credibility. Their track record has demonstrated that their opinions are worth hearing.

There is often at least one person in a group who elicits a different reaction. The group discussion might be moving along normally and then this person chimes in. Others in the group look elsewhere, fidget with objects, sometimes audibly sigh. Though it's not good manners, sometimes they mutter to one another and roll their eyes. Why? Because this person has no credibility with the group. What he or she has to say might be true and helpful, but it doesn't matter to the others. They don't want to hear it.

The basis of credibility

Where does credibility come from? To give the broad answer, let's revisit the concept of your Leadership Effect.

$$\begin{array}{ccc} \textbf{Professional Competence} & & \\ \textbf{(Knowledge \& Skills)} & & \textbf{Your} \\ \textbf{+} & \textbf{=} & \textbf{Leadership} \\ \textbf{Personal Conduct} & & \textbf{Effect} \\ \textbf{(Behaviors)} & & \end{array}$$

We have already seen that professional competence is necessary to build your Leadership Effect. Many individuals in business or other pursuits have squandered their credibility by failing at the competence side of the table. That is often the reason behind the slumps, sighs, and rolling eyes.

Though necessary, professional competence is not sufficient to be a successful leader. It is usually on the behavior side of the chart that people succeed or fail in building leadership credibility.

What kind of effect do you have on the people who work around you? Do you have a positive effect, raising others' attitudes and moods? Or do you have a negative effect, demotivating and pulling the group down to discouragement? Do you raise people's sights to see purpose and value in your work? Or do you focus on what is wrong and breed complaining and blaming? Do you speak well of the organization and its people? Or are you a master at pinpointing everyone's faults and failures?

You can be sure of this: You have an effect on others who spend time around you. If you want to successfully win followers, you must be constantly aware of the effect you are producing on others through your attitudes, words, and actions.

Leaders create positive environments in their presence. That's essential for credibility.

Behavior breakdowns cost credibility

Let's return to Lawrence as an example. When I was called in to work with him, I went through my usual pattern of inquiry. How did he rate in terms of professional competence? Couldn't be much higher. Everyone from the CEO to peers to those below him agreed that Lawrence knew the business inside out, and his integrity and work ethic were excellent.

I moved on to our irreducible definition of leadership, part one: Did he know where he was going? Could he articulate in a leadership context what he wanted? Again, no problem at all. The CEO said Lawrence "is driven by goals and priorities, then he lasers in on them."

And yet, there was this persistent theme that people didn't enjoy working with him.

The problem had to be located in part two of our irreducible definition, Lawrence's "ability to persuade others to go along with him." If it was not in the area of clear goals and objectives, the problem had to be in the realm of behavior.

One theme I heard several times was that Lawrence had a habit of popping out with opinions or pronouncements that felt cutting to others. He would assertively state his view of things and walk away, leaving people offended or hurt. Interestingly, whenever Lawrence was made aware of this, he quickly and sincerely apologized. It grieved him to discover he had hurt someone. It just seemed he was usually unaware of it unless they spoke up.

As I listened to people and sifted through written feedback, certain themes were mentioned repeatedly. The following are excerpts of real comments from others answering the question, "How can Lawrence be more effective?" Here's your chance to be a coach. What do you hear directly and between the lines of their responses, and how would you advise Lawrence?

"Practice patience …"

"… by building stronger relationships with direct and indirect subordinates …"

"By being more open-minded … It takes slowing down and walking you through his mind to grasp certain ideas or initiatives."

"Listen more, talk less."

"Listen more, think through a response and give it more time."

"He needs to develop better questioning and listening skills."

"Don't jump to conclusions."

Lawrence was a classic case; one I run into routinely coaching successful people: His greatest strengths were simultaneously his greatest weaknesses.

How strengths can become weaknesses

That may sound strange to you, but follow me here. When Lawrence and I worked to build a functional model of him (stage one of my coaching process), it was obvious that two of his greatest strengths that helped explain his success were being results-oriented and an extremely fast mental processor.

Lawrence lived his entire life, professionally and personally, around identifying objectives and getting results. That's good, if we're talking about the most important things. Professionally, that trait had much to do with his success. It provided the never-resting drive to achieve and succeed. Recall the CEO's comment that he "is driven by goals and priorities, then he lasers in on them."

However, he also admitted to me that he tended to apply this trait automatically to trivial things. His chronic impatience in driving a car stemmed from the fact that he had set a goal of arriving at his destination at a certain time, even when it didn't really matter. Any delays encountered in traffic were hindering him from his goal, and that drove him crazy.

This also helped me understand how someone with strong moral values and who genuinely cared for people could have a bad habit of making cutting comments. It wasn't that he didn't care about people's feelings. He just lost sight of them due to his laser focus on the goal to be achieved. For Lawrence, all he could see at any given moment was the bulls-eye on the current target.

His second pitfall was that of being an extremely fast mental processor. Many people are not aware of this subject, so let me briefly explain. We all process at different speeds and methods. If you imagine a scale with "extremely fast" on one end and "slow systematic" on the other, we all fit in there somewhere. Keep in mind this is about HOW someone processes new information or situations, not about intelligence. Some of the most intelligent people I've ever known are on the slow systematic end of the scale.

Both sides have pluses and minuses. The most important applications are, first, understanding yourself, how you process and the potential strengths and weaknesses it can lead to; second, understanding that other people process differently, and keeping that in mind as you interact with them. You must respect other people's different ways of processing rather than insisting they do it your way or writing them off as "difficult."

This understanding is particularly important when leading meetings. Fast processors must beware of making snap judgments or trying to push through new material too rapidly. If they don't relax enough to allow their slower teammates to think through items, many in the group will push back. Slower processors must take care to be prepared and do their processing *before* the meeting. They should not try to do their processing in the meeting. Otherwise, they can frustrate the faster, action-oriented teammates, who are rolling their eyes and saying, "Can we please *get on* with it?"

Lawrence's warp speed in thought and action had all kinds of unintended consequences. He would speak early in conversations and shut them down. He would drop cutting opinions and walk away, thinking about the next objective. He visibly showed his impatience in meetings when things or conversations were not moving fast enough for him (which they never were). His subordinates were often left in the dust, bewildered and not understanding what was happening or what to do.

Strengths can become weaknesses when they are unconsciously and automatically applied; that is, when we don't know when to dial them down or turn them off. Weaknesses are often strengths on overdrive.

Awareness enables change

Becoming aware of these dynamics for the first time, Lawrence understood that most of the negative effects could be traced back to hyper-focus and speed. He simply had to learn to broaden his focus and recognize situations where he needed to slow down. His high moral values and ideals provided all the motivation he needed to work to change. Now gaining greater self-awareness, he worked with me to build processes, reminders, and new habits to ensure he slowed down and connected with people. Sincerely wanting to grow and change, he did.

He embraced the value of taking time with people, helping them get up to speed and clarifying his thinking and expectations. One phrase that helped him was, "Go slow now to go fast later." Taking time for people now became an investment that allowed for future speed, which he found motivating.

Months later, people were pleasantly surprised by his improvement. Lawrence could not change his basic make-up (no one can), but he could and did gain *greater self-awareness* and learn new habits of *behavior*. He is a much better listener today, and, most importantly, his leadership credibility has risen in the eyes of others.

Your Credibility Bank Account

Having discussed and illustrated credibility as the currency of leadership, we still must find a way to get our arms around it. How can you measure it?

For many years, at least as far back as the 1980s, I have used a model to help people to apply this issue: a **Credibility Bank Account**. I didn't invent this concept and am not sure who actually was first to use it, having seen it in many sources. I have developed my own approach to teaching and applying it that I use with coaching clients and training groups.

Here's the concept: You have, in the minds of potential followers, an imaginary bank account with a credibility balance that rises and falls based on their opinion of you. Over time your behavior makes deposits, adding to your credibility in their eyes, or withdrawals, diminishing your leadership influence over them.

Let's say you can potentially have up to 100 credibility bucks in your account. That would mean absolute perfection and complete unquestioned trust in the minds of others. Of course, no one is perfect, so that's an unattainable ideal. On the other end, it's theoretically possible that you have zero credibility bucks in your account in the eyes of others. That would mean you are absolutely bankrupt in terms of credibility.

The higher your credibility rating, the more you can successfully call people to follow you. The more difficult, challenging, or uncomfortable the thing you are asking people to do, the more credibility bucks it costs you, and the higher balance you must have. If, for example, you have 88 credibility bucks in your account, people are likely to follow you even if it costs them something. If, on the other hand, you have 28 credibility bucks in your account, not a chance.

Once familiar with this metaphorical approach, several things jump out at you:

- **Anything you do that reduces your credibility with your followers reduces your power to lead**

Lawrence's story illustrates how a large amount of acknowledged strengths can be undermined by small behaviors, thus diminishing one's Leadership Effect.

If people will choose or not choose to follow you based on your credibility in their eyes, you can see that *anything* you do that reduces that credibility must be avoided. This is the blind spot of those who rely solely on professional competence to enable them to lead. In the last chapter, I gave two bad examples, Stu the director and Dr. Bill the surgeon. Both of them thought their bad behavior could be dismissed because they were so good on the competence side. They deceived only themselves.

It's amazing how people can rationalize or deny away obvious bad habits or behaviors, thinking, "After all, look at all the good I do. What does being on time ... speaking to others courteously ... being a cooperative teammate have to do with my top-level knowledge and skills?" Behaviors like those *don't* have much to do with knowledge and skills. They do have everything to do with building and establishing your leadership credibility.

We all have weaknesses and faults that cause us to leak credibility, requiring continuous deposits.

Everyone, no exceptions, has strengths and weaknesses, along with an assortment of quirks, idiosyncrasies, and undesirable habits. Believe me, the people who live and work around you could list yours in a minute! Therefore, your credibility bank balance is like a bucket with a hole in it. You are constantly leaking credibility just because you are an ordinary human being. That means you must dedicate yourself to making continuous deposits *just to stay even.*

- **Good behaviors do not negate major faults**

Dr. Bill, you'll remember, had a bad tendency to blow up and blister people way out of bounds. When he was confronted about it, he said something like this: "But I'm really a nice person! Yes, there have been a couple times when I lost my temper, but it's not like it's happened that often. I think I'm friendly and likeable most of the time."

It's amazing how many people think this way. My response is to laugh and offer an illustration: Imagine I rob a bank and get caught. I protest to the policeman putting me in handcuffs, "But this isn't fair! I only robbed one bank! There are thirty-one days in the month, and I only robbed a bank *today.* What about the thirty days I *didn't* rob a bank? Don't I get any credit for those?"

No, there are certain faults and bad behaviors that can negate a mountain of good behavior. We all have faults and will fall short of the ideal, but we must at all costs avoid the kinds of faults that will blow a hole in the bottom of our bank balance. It doesn't take very long to make a mistake you will long regret. Continual self-awareness and self-management is a necessity for any would-be leader.

- **Your leadership credibility requires constant attention**

The chapters ahead will give you many angles on building your leadership credibility. Also, in **Part III** you'll find methods to measure yourself and identify areas in which you want to improve, plus a web address from which you can download my Leadership Self-Assessment. For now, the most important thing is to recognize the absolute critical importance of this subject for any aspiring leader.

If you want to lead, it must become your constant concentration to *build* and *protect* your leadership credibility.

You can't afford to take days, hours, or even minutes off. "When can I just be myself?" many people ask. I reply, "If you mean, 'When can you just say and do whatever comes naturally without running it through your leadership filter?' the answer is NEVER."

People are watching, and your attitudes, words, and actions are always on display. Careless words and actions can drop your credibility level quickly. This is a critical part of "the will to *prepare* to lead" we examined in the last chapter.

I hope you gather many helpful insights from this book, but if there's only one thing you take away — just ONE thing — I urge you to take away Leadership Proposition 1:

The *Currency* of Leadership Is *Credibility*

Your success as a leader depends on it!

Leading Insights

Part II: Proposition 1
The *Currency* of Leadership Is *Credibility*

- People will follow you for two reasons:
    1. Because of their trust or confidence in you
    2. Because they believe the future will be better if they do

- Credibility is the currency of leadership. With sufficient credibility, you can successfully call people to follow you.

- Effective leaders create positive environments in their presence. That's essential for building credibility.

- Strengths become weaknesses when they are unconsciously or automatically applied; when you don't know when to dial them down or turn them off.

- You have a Credibility Bank Account balance in the minds of your followers, which rises and falls based on your behavior. Implications:
    1. Anything you do that lessens your credibility reduces your power to lead
    2. We all have weaknesses and faults that cause us to leak credibility, requiring continuous deposits
    3. Good behaviors do not negate major faults

Leadership Proposition 2
The *Goal* of Leadership Is
A Better Future

O n August 28, 1963, a man stood on the steps of the Lincoln Memorial and spoke for 17 minutes. He was listed number sixteen out of eighteen presentations on the official program.

Seventeen minutes.

His 17 minute address has been selected as the greatest American speech of the 20th century. A quarter of a million people were present to hear his words, which have continued to resonate and inspire millions to this day and surely will continue to do so into the future.

His name was Martin Luther King, Jr. What was it he said that has carried such power and inspired so many?

"I have a dream ..."

Dr. King painted a verbal picture of an America that lives up to her stated ideal: "that all men are created equal." He spoke of a United States where children of different races would play together without consciousness of their differences; where former adversaries could sit and eat together in fellowship; and where all men and women and boys and girls would be judged according to the content of their character rather than the color of their skin.

Dr. King understood human nature and the yearnings of the human heart that are common to mankind. He understood the power of *hope*. And he understood that effective leadership is fueled by imparting a vision that the future can and will be **BETTER**.

"Why should I follow you?"

Potential followers will ask, "Why should I follow you?" I have asserted previously that people choose to follow a leader for one or both of two reasons:

1. Because of their trust in the leader, his or her credibility
2. Because they believe the future will be better if they do

Our first two propositions flow directly from these:

Leadership Proposition 1: **The *Currency* of Leadership Is *Credibility***
Leadership Proposition 2: **The *Goal* of Leadership Is *a Better Future***

Without belief in your credibility, people are not likely to follow you. In the same way, people are not likely to follow you if they don't believe that if they do the future will in some way be better. They might follow you if there is only one of these reasons present, but it's far better to have both.

If only the first is present — people trust *you*, but they can't see how following will lead to a better future — they might still follow, but you are at risk. Your message to them is essentially, "I know you can't see what I see, *but trust me.*"

People will follow in such a case only if you have a high credibility balance in their eyes. They might follow easily the first time, but after a disappointment people will follow, if at all, with more suspicion and scrutiny. If you ask for people's blind trust and the effort seriously fails, it will cost you dearly in terms of credibility. It will take a long time to dig out of that hole.

On the other hand, if only the second is present — followers believe the picture you paint of future benefits, but you have a low credibility rating — they might choose to follow, but their motives are likely to be selfish and, again, there will be greater suspicion and scrutiny. There will be a "what's in it for me?" attitude. People are quick to abandon a leader with low credibility after a failure.

But where you have both, as in the example of Dr. King — a man of very high moral authority and credibility, along with a powerful gift of communicating his vision of an ideal future — the effect can be electrifying. People by the thousands can be mobilized around a shared vision and motivated to apply effort, dedication, and focus, even to the point of enduring hardship and danger.

A powerful universal motivator

There are some things that are universal, across all the usual barriers that divide human beings. We are all stirred and moved when HOPE is aroused in us.

According to the dictionary, hope is "a feeling that what is wanted will happen" and "desire accompanied by expectation." Interestingly, the root meaning of the word in the ancient languages was related to the verb "to hop." Therefore, the original concept of the word meant something like "to leap up in expectation."

I like that definition, because that is what hope feels like. When a leader speaks and taps into this need, people say things like, "My heart leaped in my chest." They sit up in their chairs, lock eyes on the speaker, and open themselves to what is being said.

In 1959 Vince Lombardi was named head coach of the woeful Green Bay Packers, a team that had won exactly *one game* the year before.

How would the new coach lead the way to improvement? Would he try to win two? Four? Half their games? This is what Lombardi said in his first team meeting:

Gentlemen, we are going to relentlessly chase *perfection* — knowing full well we will not catch it because nothing is perfect. But we are going to relentlessly chase it because in the process we will catch *excellence*.

"Perfection"? "Excellence"? How about rising to "average"? Or, at least "not stinking"? For this team, becoming "pretty good" seemed beyond possibility. No, Lombardi knew that small plans do not inflame the minds of men. After saying the above, he paused and moved within reaching distance of the first row of players. Lombardi then added with conviction:

I am not remotely interested in just being "good."[1]

Quarterback Bart Starr was so excited that he immediately ran to a phone to call his wife back in Alabama, exclaiming, "We're going to begin to win!" And they did, winning five NFL championships in the next nine years.

Those who played for Lombardi describe him consistently as a master psychologist. He looked at his players as individuals and treated them accordingly. He always knew which ones needed a tough driver, and which ones needed a gentle touch. In that opening speech, he also displays his knowledge of what is universal in human nature, connecting with deep human yearnings that move people to achieve great things.

How to touch human hearts

In every human heart are certain desires that wise leaders recognize and tap into in order to inspire people to follow and achieve. Though for many people these desires are buried under a deep pile of discouragement, they are still there with the potential to be fanned into a flame. Here are three things you can assume for almost anyone you meet.

1. A hunger for encouragement

This is a world of disappointments. All of us have experienced a degree of them. Some people feel they have been bludgeoned by a relentless stream of disappointments. We regret that we have not achieved what we dreamed. We have watched peers climb up and up, while we thrash around below. Our marriages or children have not turned out as we wished. We struggle with self-discipline in our personal and professional lives. Other people seem to be happier and more confident.

What does this mean to a leader? You can know one of the simplest things you can do to earn leadership influence with others. I urge you to adopt this philosophy: There is never enough encouragement in the world.

Therefore: **Become an encourager.**

I taught this philosophy to my children when they were growing up. Like most young people, they wanted to learn the secret of popularity. I told them, "There is never enough encouragement in the world. People are hungry for it. If you make it your aim to go around encouraging other people, you will always be welcome."

That's a good word for anyone who aspires to lead. It does much more than make you more popular. It marks you as a leader.

Encourage people *by expressing your confidence in them.* I've said it countless times in coaching sessions: "I believe in you. You can do this." It's amazing how powerful those words can be.

Encourage people *by refocusing their attention when they are down.* Remind them of the benefits and positive results they are striving for.

Encourage people *by recognizing them for the good they do.* Recognition and appreciation are two of the most powerful of the basic motivators, and effective leaders use them liberally. They function like oil and water in your car, reducing friction and heat, and allowing people to continue functioning smoothly and keep pressing on.

2. "To BE better than I am, and to DO better than I have before"

Most of us have a list of things we wish we had achieved or could do better: earn a promotion, break a bad habit, be a better parent, lose weight, be more self-disciplined, be better organized, exercise regularly, and so on. We wrestle with our weaknesses and limitations, and strain to apply self-control. This is where a leader can be immensely powerful. You can awaken the echoes of those inner desires and rekindle hope that *it could be.* Leaders have the ability to help people believe that change and growth are possible.

However, we often need the help of a coach, mentor, teacher, trainer, or leader in order to approach our potential. We need that person who cares enough about us to be hard on us in a caring way. Lombardi's players are nearly unanimous in reporting that while he was extremely demanding, he genuinely cared about them. Fifty years later, they still speak with gratitude about the dominant positive influence he was in their lives, teaching life lessons that went way beyond football.

That's why effective leaders don't aim to make things easy for their followers. They know that, while most of us wrestle with areas of self-discipline and inertia, we are motivated by the desire to be **BETTER** than we are. This is what Lombardi's contemporary, Coach Tom Landry, had in mind when he gave this definition of his job:

> A head coach is someone who makes a player do what he does not want to do in order to achieve what he wants to achieve.

I have often asked leadership and managing classes about the people who most influenced their lives. They quickly name parents, sports coaches, previous managers, or spiritual leaders who helped them learn and grow. I ask next, "Were those leaders easy on you?" and I usually get lots of laughter in return. Almost to a person, they testify that those influential leaders were truthful and demanding, regularly pushing them beyond their comfort zones. It was clear, though, that this pushing came out of genuine concern for them and their development.

Those people are forever grateful to leaders who inspired them to be and do beyond what they could have achieved on their own.

3. "To be part of something greater than myself"

World-changing individuals have been visionaries who led movements: William Wilberforce working to end the slave trade in the British Empire; Gandhi leading his people to nonviolently win India's independence; Martin Luther King contending for full civil rights for African-Americans in the United States.

Each of these worked for *years* toward their vision, beginning with few followers but eventually winning thousands of partners. In his own way, each changed the world.

Effective leaders of movements know that in every human heart are certain deep desires, especially the desire "to be part of something greater than myself." It doesn't have to be on a national scale like the leaders I've mentioned. Any organization that has a *meaningful* mission, vision, and values has the potential to raise its employees or members beyond the level of "selling widgets to make bucks." The mission can be something *great* if it's taken seriously.

Twice I have been in a position to lead an organizational turn-around. In 1991 I was asked to step in as Executive Director and Chairman of the Board for a nonprofit public service organization, the Christian Concern Foundation. CCF had a long and influential history, going back to the 1970s. However, it lost Creath Davis, its founder and leader, in 1987 in a tragic plane crash. Others tried to carry on the work without success. CCF was on its last legs. Before I began discussions with them, the board had been seriously considering shutting it down.

The first thing I did was to meet with the staff, active volunteer members, and long-time supporters. What could I say? How could I help this group of people regain a sense of hope and belief that we could have a meaningful future? Here is an outline of that first talk:

- First, I recalled the long and fruitful track record CCF had produced. I acknowledged many in the room who were important contributors of those good works.

- I recalled the loss of Creath Davis, a man they deeply loved and respected. The grief they still felt years later was real and should be acknowledged. I then went on to discuss what I appreciated about his values, character, and dedication. I encouraged a discussion where others shared what they felt about his legacy.

- I then spoke of myself. I shared with them my own values and aspirations. "I would never claim to be gifted as greatly, or in the same ways, as Creath," I told them, "but I am ready to pick up this work and dedicate myself to the vision we share."

- I then described the **future** as I pictured it. To me it was a vision full of purpose, meaningful service, and life-changing results for many people. "We have a real reason to exist," I told them, "if we will rededicate ourselves to pursuing these God-given purposes. I am asking you to join me."

They did. Within a short time, we were fully functioning, and CCF was back on its feet. The staff and volunteers were again positive, believing in our work and in our future. When I left a few years later to assume leadership of another organization, CCF was positioned for many more years of service.

These universal motivators are the secret to winning people to deep and long-term commitments. I have suggested previously that you don't have to be especially charismatic to be an effective leader, that many great leaders in history have been charisma-challenged. So how did they win passionate followers? It was because *the charisma was in their **ideas**, not themselves*. If you can paint mental pictures for people that touch on these universal human yearnings, you can engage powerful motives that move others.

Leaders are future-oriented

Recalling our working definition, how can you know if you are a leader? You are a leader if you know where you are going and are able to persuade others to go along with you. Add to that the bare dictionary definition: Leadership is "the ability to lead." While that may seem unhelpful, I pointed out earlier that "to lead" is a verb, implying action.

"Where you are going" obviously pictures someone going somewhere. That means motion, a direction, and a goal. Leaders are about what's ahead, about how the **future** will be **BETTER**.

There is some value in focusing on the past. Chiefly, to learn lessons useful for the future: What went wrong? Why did it go wrong? What were the conditions or influences that led to an undesirable effect? You've probably heard the popular definition of insanity: "Doing the same thing over and over again while expecting a different result." Another bit of wisdom regarding the past is found in a well-known saying: "Those who do not remember the past are doomed to repeat it."

I believe in reflecting on past experiences, but effective leaders are never preoccupied with the past. The greatest value of doing so is the ability to make better choices in the future.

Visualizing a better future

The process of leading begins with the question, "What do you want?" followed by, "Do you want to *do* something about it?" A better future can begin now.

"Future" is very broad. It can refer to:
- A problem you want to fix this afternoon
- The creation of an improved state, such as a better functioning team
- A long-term development project
- The turn-around of an organization
- An unachievable ideal you will pursue for a lifetime

However near or remote, you must be thinking ahead in order to lead. You must "know where you are going" before you can "persuade others to go along with you."

In discussions of these things, I've had people respond to me with, "I don't know. I'm no visionary."

We tend to apply the term "visionary" to people who are uniquely gifted at seeing a long-term and grand picture of the future. This is one of those categories in which we are not created equal. There are world-class leaders who can imagine and strategize literally decades into the future. That kind of ability is very rare. More conventional leaders can imagine a few years ahead. Many people seem to lack any ability at all in this area, though it may be they just don't want to exert the effort required for hard thinking.

There is actually some danger involved in being a gifted visionary. I worked with a CEO who was exceptional in this way. Carol could see what was coming in her business field long before most others. She was truly amazing in her strategic ability, and it enabled her company to jump several years ahead of their competitors. The only problem was that she often forgot that others couldn't see what she could see. She was sometimes so far out in front of her followers that they became bewildered and confused.

There's a word of warning I often share with leaders:

Two steps ahead of the people equals a leader. Ten steps ahead of the people equals a martyr.

People who can think years ahead must remember that they're working chiefly with the less gifted and ungifted, people who can't imagine a fraction of the vision they see. If they forget to back up to where their followers are when communicating, they can lose them. In extreme cases, visionaries can find themselves out of a job.

If you have that visionary ability, it's a valuable gift and a great advantage for you as a leader. You just have to remember that you can't communicate that far in front of others. Even though the vision is clear to *you*, it isn't clear to *them*. At most, like Martin Luther King, Jr., you can paint a picture of a remote ideal future that touches hearts. But in describing the next actions you want from them, you must back up closer to where they are. Clearly describe the next few steps that are within their ability, and they'll willingly follow.

Answer the questions currently on their minds

You don't have to spend time trying to figure out if you're a visionary right now. The most important questions in the minds of your followers are along these lines:

- Can you imagine a better future? How so? What might it look like?
- Can you imagine the next steps that could move us that way?
- Are there any obstacles or problems we might face?
- Where do I fit in? What do other individuals bring to the table that can be helpful in this process?

And remember to consider their big questions:

- What *encouragement* can you offer to raise our hopes that things can be better?
- In what ways can you tap into our inborn desire *to be and do better* than we have done before?
- How might this effort be connected to *something greater* than ourselves?

If you can articulate your thoughts to questions like these, you are ready to lead to a better future.

This is a good place to recall something I said in the second chapter. This does not mean you have to know all the answers, by any means! In fact, some of the most important leadership examples in the world begin when *nobody* knows what to do, but some man or woman speaks up and says, "We have to do something about this. There must be a way to make this better. Let's go to work."

A group of well-meaning, intelligent people can do wonders when their hopes are raised and they are inspired to put their heads together, attack a problem, and make things **BETTER**.

That's what leaders do.

The leader made the difference

I'd like to close this chapter by returning to Vince Lombardi and the 1959 Green Bay Packers, the team who went on to win five NFL championships in nine years.

If my count is correct, that team which had won only one game in 1958 contained *seven players* who eventually were elected to the NFL Hall of Fame.

They were already there, on a team that went 1-10-1.

Think about that. What made the difference?

Leadership.

Leading Insights

Part II: Proposition 2
The *Goal* of Leadership Is *a Better Future*

- Effective leadership is fueled by imparting a vision that the future can and will be better.

- We are all stirred and moved when hope is aroused in us.

- To motivate, wise leaders tap into universal desires of the human heart:
    1. A hunger for encouragement
    2. "To BE better than I am, and to DO better than I have before"
    3. "To be part of something greater than myself"

- Effective leaders learn from the past, but they are never preoccupied with it.

- You must be thinking ahead in order to lead, and be able to articulate clearly your vision or goal.

Leadership Proposition 3
The *Attitude* of Leadership Is *Optimism*

People will follow you if they have confidence in your credibility and they believe the future can be better than today. Now you face a really big question: Do YOU believe it?

Optimism is your belief and determination that things can and will be **BETTER**. In any given situation, you can be sure that many people do not believe that. They are the ones saying:

"We'll never make it."

"Our situation is hopeless."

"We'll never get out of this."

"We're doomed."

Would you follow someone with those attitudes? Of course not. They have nothing to offer. People who think and speak like that cannot lead.

What is the opposite of a leader? I believe that if you ask a number of average people this question, the most common answer will be, "a follower." That is not true. Marcus Buckingham has rightly observed:

> Properly defined, the opposite of a leader isn't a follower. The opposite of a leader is a *pessimist*.[1]

Take that to heart. In a time of discouragement, challenge, trouble, or crisis, people look to the person who says, "C'mon, we can do this. What can we do to fix it … make things better … work our way out of this?" That's why one of our fundamental principles is Leadership Proposition 3: **The *Attitude* of Leadership Is *Optimism*.**

There's just one problem: What does the word "optimism" mean? Based on my experience, this is the proposition that requires more clarification than any other.

"What do you mean by that?"

Have you ever noticed that in a controversy people often seem to get nowhere? Whether the category is politics, philosophy, or theology, two or more people can get locked in a debate for hours without resolving anything.

One of the most common reasons is this: They are using the same terms, but unknowingly meaning something different by them. Comically, if they were to realize the difference in the definitions of the words they are using, they would often quickly see that they really aren't that far apart on the issue at all, that they've been shooting past each other. The hours of debate (and often, bad feelings) were a waste of time and energy. This happens all the time in media debates about politics and policy. On the other hand, they might discover that there really is a difference of opinion and understand where each other is coming from.

That's why I have taught people for years this bit of wisdom: At the beginning of any controversy, before you wade in, ask: "What do you mean by that?"

Example: Someone asks you, "Are you a liberal or a conservative?" Before you answer, ask, "What do you mean by 'liberal' and 'conservative'? Can you give me your definition of those words?" Here's how three hypothetical individuals might answer.

Person 1 says, "A liberal tends to support a bigger government as the answer to our social problems, and a conservative believes in a smaller government with the private sector being the best means to address those problems."

Person 2 says, "A liberal is someone who cares for the poor and disadvantaged, and a conservative is a hard-hearted, bigoted rich person who only cares about himself."

Person 3 says, "A liberal is a bleeding-heart thieving socialist, and a conservative is someone with sound common sense and who believes in a good work ethic."

Can you see what kind of trouble you can get yourself into by answering a question without making sure you know what the questioner means by their terms? If you hold a leadership position, people will bring you questions all the time. Sometimes they will be honest questions arising from curiosity, ignorance, or insecurity. Sometimes they will be loaded questions posed by opponents, skeptics, or resistors.

So let me offer you a valuable bit of leadership advice: Work hard at training yourself not to "shoot from the lip"; that is, to speak impulsively without reflecting on the possible ramifications of conversations. Get into the habit of asking, "What do you mean by that?" Make sure you understand what he or she is thinking and means by their question before offering an answer.

This simple practice can save you a whole lot of headache! Plus, thinking through what you mean by the terms you use prepares you for clear and powerful communication with potential followers.

What is the meaning of "optimism"?

We now apply that principle to the subject of this chapter. I have asserted that the attitude of leadership is optimism, but what does that word mean? How can you know if you are an optimist? As you might suspect, those words mean different things to different people. To progress, we must clear away several counterfeits.

- Some write off optimists as naïve Pollyannas who don't see the world as it is.
- Some think optimists ignore or deny reality, especially negative facts.
- Some think optimism is about wishful thinking, that things will somehow magically get better by themselves.
- Some equate optimism with a positive attitude.

The term "positive attitude" is problematic in itself, however. It also has a wide range of possible meanings to different people. Therefore, if I am asked if optimism means the same thing as a positive attitude, I respond, "It depends. What do you mean by a 'positive attitude'?"

It can mean the same thing as my definition of optimism.

A positive attitude can also mean an unrealistic determination not to look at or talk about negative truths. Many a company or organization has gotten into deep trouble, in fact, because of an unspoken cultural value that "we don't talk about negative things here." But not talking about them doesn't make them go away, and the consequences can be major.

A positive attitude can also be a code term for a whole metaphysical philosophy (which I thoroughly reject) that holds that you can actually create reality through your "mental power" of a "positive mental attitude." If that's what someone means by a positive attitude, no, it is not what I mean by optimism.

Some believe optimism equates to manufactured excitement.

Dr. Howard Hendricks liked to tell a story about the fictional Fido Dog Food Company. They held a large meeting of their Marketing and Sales Departments, and the speaker was revving up the crowd.

"WHO HAS THE BEST MARKETING STRATEGY?" he shouted.
"WE DO!" the crowd answered.
"WHO HAS THE BEST SALES TEAM?"
"WE DO!"
"WHO HAS THE BEST PACKAGING?"
"WE DO!"

The leader leaned on the podium and asked in a flat voice: "Then why do we rank number 17 out of 19 dog food companies?"

A little voice from the back of the ballroom answered: "Because dogs don't like us."

Emotions and excitement don't change reality.

People are not committed to excellent performance just because they mouth the right responses. It's amazing to me how many managers are satisfied with an outward show of excitement and enthusiasm. Effective leaders can stimulate people to bring willing commitment to the task through the substance of their credibility and message.

Optimism is not the same as hype, getting people excited. Optimism is not primarily about the emotions at all. Excitement is of little value in leadership because it has a short shelf life and offers little resistance against negative reality. But belief that the future can be better, along with persistence, determination, and drive can lead people there.

The character of genuine optimism

Optimism is the belief and determination that the future can and will be better despite the obstacles or difficulties we must endure.

Notice: There is no denial of negative reality here. There is a clear acknowledgement of the problems, difficulties, or challenges ahead while remaining confident of the ultimate outcome. That is genuine optimism. That is also what I mean when I refer to a positive attitude. Attacking the negative can sometimes be the most positive thing you can do.

What keeps leaders from openly identifying and attacking problems? Some fear the disturbance and turmoil that are generated by pointing out difficulties. Some fear the pressure of people's attempts at work avoidance, because addressing and solving problems often requires sustained, focused effort. Some simply fear telling the truth. We must accept the fact that speaking the truth is an integral characteristic of principled leadership and inseparable from genuine optimism.

On May 13, 1940, Winston Churchill accepted the position of Prime Minister of Great Britain. Circumstances were dire. France was being overrun, leaving the British to stand alone against the Nazi war machine. The United States would continue to maintain neutrality until the end of 1941. Months and months would pass without a victory in battle. Ahead was the Battle of Britain, daily bombing of English cities with widespread death and destruction. The English people lived in fear of an imminent German invasion of their island.

How would you like to become leader in a time like that? What would you say in your opening talk to your people? Should you downplay the bad news? Is this the time for positive thinking? Should you rev up some excitement?

This is what Churchill said in his first address to Parliament and the British people:

I would say to the House, as I said to those who've joined this government: "I have nothing to offer but blood, toil, tears, and sweat."

We have before us an ordeal of the most grievous kind. We have before us many, many long months of struggle and of suffering.

Does that sound optimistic to you?

The truth is, that's what people want to hear when there's bad news. They commonly ask, "How bad is it?" They want to know the worst, and they want it straight. When leaders try to downplay negative facts or casually surf over them, followers are quick to pick up on it. The people know better. Leaders lose credibility when they try to dance around negative truth.

You should take to heart something Churchill said on a different occasion:

There is no worse mistake in public leadership than to hold out false hope soon to be swept away.

Churchill did not hold out false hope on this occasion, nor on any other, but he did not stop there with the bad news. He went on to say:

You ask, what is our policy? I will say: It is to wage war, by sea, land, and air, with all our might and with all the strength that God can give us; to wage war against a monstrous tyranny, never surpassed in the dark and lamentable catalogue of human crime. That is our policy. You ask, what is our aim? I can answer in one word: victory. Victory at all costs, victory in spite of all terror, victory, however long and hard the road may be; for without victory, there is no survival.

"Victory"? There had been no successes at all to date, just repeated humiliating capitulations. At this time, there were many in Britain who believed their only way out was a negotiated settlement with Hitler. Churchill wouldn't entertain the thought. Notice his unvarnished description of the Nazis in the paragraph above. No, despite the long ordeal of suffering and sacrifice ahead, he clearly identified victory as their only appropriate objective.

He concluded his brief remarks with this:

But I take up my task with buoyancy and hope. I feel sure that our cause will not be suffered to fail among men. At this time, I feel entitled to claim the aid of all, and I say, "Come then, let us go forward together with our united strength."

That is genuine optimism: The belief and determination of future success despite the obstacles or difficulties we must endure.

Leadership involves risk

Few people are called upon to lead at such a critical juncture as Winston Church in 1940, but his dramatic example of optimism in spite of dire circumstances should be instructive for us who lead under more conventional conditions.

One thing you see is that Churchill took the risk of telling the English people the truth about their situation. All leadership involves risk: The risk of rejection, the risk of failure, the risk of criticism, the risk of ridicule. You are gambling on what you know about human nature, those yearnings of the human heart we saw in the last chapter: That people hunger for encouragement, to be and do better than they have done before, and to be connected with a purpose greater than themselves; that they need and will respond to a message of hope.

Many a business leader has had to rally the troops in the face of possible failure. Those who were successful communicated along the same lines as Churchill above. They started with a truthful recognition of the present difficulties, but called people to join together to meet them with determination to prevail. It often requires enduring hardship and sacrifices, but people will usually respond to such a challenge behind effective leadership.

If you have sufficient Leadership Effect through earning high credibility, those appeals will likely be successful. But also know that there are no guarantees, and that credibility, like popularity, can be fleeting. Know as well that there are times you must share bad news or disappoint people's expectations, and they won't like it. Determined optimism might be the only quality that holds your leadership influence together long enough to get things turned around.

Those that have sought to lead others to a better future have always taken these risks. The continual challenge is to squarely face the risks while maintaining an optimistic attitude.

The essential leadership attitude

Since the goal of leadership is a better future, it only makes sense that you must believe it in order to win followers. Why would anyone follow someone who doesn't believe the future can be better? Optimism is thus the essential attitude for effective leadership.

Attitudes are contagious, for good or ill. You have probably observed situations where scoffers, naysayers, and Chicken Littles crying that the sky is falling pulled an entire group down to their level. Everyone ends up sitting around in helpless paralysis whining about their lot.

You may also have observed how one person, with or without formal authority, has raised a group on his or her shoulders through force of will and belief that things can and will be better. Team members perk up, respond, and begin to pull together toward that end.

General Dwight D. Eisenhower wrote regarding his command experiences during World War II:

Optimism and pessimism are infectious and they spread more rapidly from the head downward than in any other direction.[2]

Does that mean that if you are a leader, you don't have doubts or fears? Of course not! Leaders are merely human, which means they are subject to the same assortment of insecurities, weaknesses, and wavering moods as anyone else. It is what you do with those emotions that will determine whether you enhance or deplete your leadership credibility rating.

The difference with effective leaders is that while they feel those normal emotions, they are continuously aware of their Leadership Effect and know they cannot afford to display them. Wise leaders know that followers take on their attitudes and moods, whether positive or negative, and are therefore scrupulously careful about how they carry themselves and speak. As I often warn clients, "A head cold in the captain becomes an epidemic in the crew."

Eisenhower also wrote of his growing appreciation of the commander's power of optimism, saying that it:

has a most extraordinary effect upon all with whom he comes in contact. With this clear realization, I firmly determined that my mannerisms and speech in public would always reflect the cheerful certainty of victory — that any pessimism and discouragement I might ever feel would be reserved for my pillow.[3]

Many people are uncomfortable with this discussion. "What about being myself?" they ask. "Are you saying that I have to become some kind of actor in order to be a leader?" We will deal with these questions directly when we come to Leadership Proposition 6 on the character of leadership. There we will see that it's possible to be authentic without being completely transparent.

For now let me simply respond: Whether you like it or not, this is the way the real world of human nature works. We might wish we lived in a world where, as leaders, we had the freedom to transparently display all that we think and feel, but that's not the way it is. Naïve would-be leaders who take that route find they squander away their leadership credibility. Followers may claim they want to know everything about their leader's inner reality, but once they hear it, they discover they don't like it.

Effective leaders are continuously aware of their Leadership Effect, and monitor their attitudes, words, and actions to promote the values and behaviors they want their followers to emulate.

What's yours? Glass half-full or glass half-empty?

This discussion of optimism versus pessimism is complicated by the fact that we all seem to be hard-wired one way or the other, to see the glass as half-full or half-empty. It doesn't seem possible to change our knee-jerk tendency. That means everyone has a hard time balancing this with the demands of leadership.

One of my coaching clients, Richard, is a glass-half-empty guy. He is a director-level executive, and considering that he's barely 40 years old, I anticipate several promotions in his future. He is intelligent, motivated, and gifted at strategic thinking. That's where his glass-half-empty temperament is useful. When a plan is put on the table, Richard is able to project into the future and quickly identify problems ahead. He can put his finger on the "what-about?" questions and issues that could derail the plan. Richard is a great asset to have on hand when a new plan of action is proposed.

It's just the way his brain is wired: To sort through all the practical "what-ifs?" and find potential problems ahead. It's a very good thing ... except when it's not. This quality, a strength in many contexts, was causing others to view Richard as "negative."

Richard's natural tendency to see all the potential negatives becomes a liability in a leading role. Through our coaching process, he became aware of the importance of optimism as the essential leadership attitude and learned to reign in his natural tendency to speak quickly in groups about problems. He couldn't help seeing the negatives and red flags, but he learned the importance of speaking up in an encouraging, optimistic way, knowing there would be opportunities to address the problems later. His leadership credibility has risen since he became aware of this and took steps to monitor his speech and frame his comments appropriately.

However, those natural optimists, glass-half-full types, also have some things to learn.

Jeff is one of my closest friends, as well as a long-time coaching client. He has been a gifted and successful leader since high school. Everywhere he has gone, he has led, from a college national championship team to several successful businesses. If you look up "optimist" in the dictionary, it should have Jeff's picture in there. He doesn't see problems, he sees challenges to get around, over, or through. With high confidence in his ability to win followers, Jeff expects to succeed.

A small problem with this rampant optimism emerged over time, however. Jeff has a tendency to minimize problems. He really doesn't want to acknowledge their existence. That led to some relatively small problems in his businesses growing into much larger, more serious ones.

This minimizing tendency was particularly true when relationships were involved. While he hated to face and admit this, in his super-salesman enthusiasm, he occasionally fudged and allowed people to believe what they wanted to believe. Jeff didn't actually lie to anyone, but he also didn't address little nagging comments or questions, allowing some loose ends that came back later. He just hates disappointing people, but trying to avoid doing so at all costs simply leads to disappointing them at a higher level later.

In short, Jeff shied away from the risks involved in telling the truth.

Jeff's was an out-of-balance optimism, which can be as big a hindrance as pessimism. Jeff is good-hearted and teachable, and he swallowed the coaching medicine necessary to make great strides in solving these tendencies. He worked hard at confronting his tendency to minimize negative information and facts and be more truthful with people and more forthright in addressing problems head-on.

Find your balance and be authentically optimistic

It is not possible to lead successfully if you project a negative or pessimistic appearance. On the other hand, the attempt to project optimism while minimizing or denying difficulties will also fall flat. People can see through it, and it will cost you much credibility.

Genuine optimism is your belief that the future can and will be better, in spite of the obstacles or difficulties you must face. It is the essential attitude you must have in order to win followers.

As far as expressing the attitude and mindset inherent in optimism, I love the motto of the U. S. Naval Construction Forces (the "Seabees") inscribed on their monument in Washington, D.C.:

With willing hearts and skillful hands, the difficult we do at once. The impossible takes a bit longer.

May their tribe increase!

The attitude of leadership is optimism, but keep in mind: It's easy to say you believe something. Really believing it is another thing entirely. That leads us to our next Leadership Proposition.

Leading Insights

Part II: Proposition 3
The *Attitude* of Leadership Is *Optimism*

- From the standpoint of attitude, the opposite of a leader is a pessimist.

- Optimism is the belief and determination that the future can and will be better, despite the obstacles or difficulties you must endure.

- Speaking the truth is an integral part of principled leadership, and inseparable from genuine optimism.

- All leadership involves risk. The central challenge is to squarely face the risks while maintaining an optimistic attitude.

- Attitudes are contagious, for good or ill, and proceed downward faster than any other direction. A head cold in the captain becomes an epidemic in the crew.

Leadership Proposition 4
The *Backbone* of Leadership Is *Conviction*

An ambitious student once approached the 19th century English preacher Charles Spurgeon and asked, "Sir, I am impressed with the great influence you have developed. How can I learn to gain a following as you have?"

The world-famous preacher replied, "Young man, I suggest you go out and set yourself on fire, and people will come from miles around to see you burn."

Spurgeon's answer points to a human attraction that is just as relevant in our time and in any leadership situation. In a world of hypocrisy, compromises, and sham, people are attracted to a man or woman who believes something. This is not referring to a casual check-off of what they're supposed to believe, but deep, burning, hard-as-iron *commitment* to values, philosophies, or truths that are unchangeable and nonnegotiable.

Do you know what you believe?

Do you know why you believe it?

Finally, can you pass the real test of what you believe? Will you hold to it even *if doing so costs you something?*

Only the person who will hold to their beliefs when they must pay a price for them can be said to possess convictions. Otherwise, they aren't genuine beliefs. They're only moods.

To be an effective leader you need backbone, leading us to Leadership Proposition 4: **The *Backbone* of Leadership Is *Conviction*.**

The reign of marshmallow kings

Zedekiah was an Israelite puppet king under the Babylonians in the 6th century B.C. I mention him because of this priceless description given by Eugene Peterson:

> The man was a marshmallow. He received impressions from anyone who pushed hard enough. When the pressure was off, he gradually resumed his earlier state ready for the next impression.[1]

Marshmallow kings are still with us. They are leading organizations and corporations. They are running businesses and managing offices. Some are "serving" as elected leaders of our state and national governments.

As I write this, we are deep in the midst of another Presidential election. Dozens of candidates clamor for the public's attention. This season, though, the professional commentators are baffled. Things aren't going according to the expected patterns and rules. As they try to make sense of voters' unconventional responses to the candidates, a certain theme keeps being raised. It goes along these lines: "People are sick of politics as usual. They are disgusted with both parties, and with the logjam of a dysfunctional Congress. They are sick of political correctness and with the empty posturing of talking heads willing to say anything to get themselves elected."

What we get most of the time are more examples of John Naisbitt's cynical definition: "Leadership involves finding a parade and getting in front of it."

In my opinion, this restless discontent is the public's nauseated anger at an endless string of marshmallow kings.

Marshmallow corporate values

The corporate world isn't any better. You would be hard-pressed to find a business of any size today that doesn't have a published "mission, vision, and values." Visit any corporate office and you'll likely see a framed poster with those mission, vision, and values attractively printed. Finding a company that actually takes theirs seriously is a different matter.

"Our most important asset is our people!" they proclaim. "Our employees are entitled to dignity, respect, and quality leadership." But what happens when the quarterly projections look poor? "Cut a thousand jobs," is the answer. This at the same time many executive salaries and bonuses are several hundred, sometimes a thousand, times higher than average workers are paid — even in companies that have lost money!

"We believe in excellence, ethics, and honesty," they say, but watch how they actually conduct business. *Performance* is reality, not words.

Almost all companies have stated mission, vision, and values, yes. But for too many they're just nice-sounding words on a poster or plaque. Those values sound good, but as soon as the pressure's on or there is a cost associated with abiding by them, those values are out the window. "This is the real world we're talking about," goes the sneer. "It's hard and competitive, and nice guys finish last. This isn't the place for kindergarten discussions of someone's sensitive scruples."

On July 1, 2000, the Chairman of a large American company published a 64-page Code of Ethics detailing their moral commitments. In his cover letter, the Chairman wrote,

> As officers and employees ... we are responsible for conducting the business affairs of the Company in accordance with all applicable laws and in a moral and honest manner.

Among their declared values were Respect, Integrity, Communication, and Excellence. The text included phrases like these: "We treat others as we would like to be treated ourselves ... Ruthlessness, callousness and arrogance don't belong here ... We work with customers and prospects openly, honestly, and sincerely."

Sounds pretty good, doesn't it?

The company was called Enron. Just a little more than a year later, the scandal began to break, leading to what was at the time the largest corporate bankruptcy in history. Through the use of loopholes and massive financial corruption, Enron hid billions of dollars in losses and failed deals from the public. Executives went to prison. The huge accounting firm Arthur Anderson was effectively put out of business through their association. Tens of thousands of innocent employees were thrown out of work.

That's just one notorious failure of integrity. All you have to do is to read the business news regularly to see the latest example of corporate leaders caught in lying, corruption, and fraud. And bet on it: Virtually every one of those companies has a polished statement of values.

Do you think I'm being too harsh? Try this:

Ask random people at a company if they have a mission, vision, and values statement. Chances are very high that the answer is yes.

Ask those people to recite them.

If you're really brave, ask them how the company's leadership is doing living up to them.

At the average company, you might be lucky to find one person in ten who can tell you what their company "believes." Don't be surprised if many of those employees haven't heard them mentioned since they attended an orientation class. Don't be surprised to find employees who are totally unaware that they exist at all. And if you ask the third question, be prepared for some cynical laughter.

Those mission, vision, and values are not convictions. They are marshmallow statements.

Convictions form the bones of character

Your body is equipped with bones; to be specific, an endoskeleton, meaning you wear your bones on the inside. Crabs, lobsters, and insects have an exoskeleton, meaning they wear their bones on the outside.

An endoskeleton, as we have, is a great advantage. It lends structure, allows for great strength and speed, and provides protection for vital organs (brain, heart, lungs, etc.). An endoskeleton also offers the advantage of facilitating rapid and dramatic growth. There's a reason the largest animals on earth, including elephants and whales, have endoskeletons.

Animals with exoskeletons — crabs, for example — have the advantage of greater external protection, but their hard and heavy shells make growth a difficult and limiting process. That's why you've never seen an elephant-sized lobster.

Convictions form the bones of character. These are not merely opinions, moods, or verbal assents to beliefs, but genuine commitments. Like bones, they are meant to be strong, hard, and unyielding. It is their unchanging nature that allows for flexibility, strength, and personal growth. They also provide the basis for setting boundaries in several directions.

The best and most enduring leaders possess convictions, which provide structure, strength, and direction as they lead followers and continue to grow themselves. Convictions about what? Here are three major categories:

1. Personal Convictions: Fundamental human questions

There are questions common to the human race:
- "Who am I?" Our need for identity
- "Why am I here?" Our desire for meaning and purpose in life
- "What makes me significant?" We want our lives to matter
- "Where can I belong?" Our need for love and acceptance, to be part of a group

There are many ways, healthy and unhealthy, that people try to answer these questions for themselves. Having personal convictions regarding these issues is critical for facing the onslaught of decisions we must make in an average day. Acting contrary to what we believe creates tremendous internal conflict and results in a life careening off-course.

The defining moment in my life occurred in February 1978 when I became a believer and dedicated follower of Jesus Christ. This was after an extended period of active inquiry as a reluctant (even hostile) skeptic. I have found clear answers for myself to those fundamental questions through Christ.

You may not be a person of my faith or any faith. I maintain, however, that you still must face those questions. They are basic needs of the human heart.

2. Principle Convictions: Your sense of right and wrong

You and I will have countless opportunities in the course of a week to do the right or wrong thing. Given the pressures, temptations, and influences all around us, waiting until the moment of crisis to try to figure out what we believe is not likely to end well.

As a Christian, most of these questions are settled for me by the teachings of the Bible, my plumb line of truth. Since the only acceptable standard of Christian living is the perfect character of Christ himself, I freely admit I have fallen short of this ideal every day of my life, as has every other Christian. But the standard is clear, unchanging, and not debatable for me. I will simply get up today and try again to do better.

If you're not a person of faith, you're not off the hook. You still know right from wrong. How do I know that? Because *everybody does*. This isn't the place to go into sophisticated philosophical arguments, but I can demonstrate it simply: The proof that you know right from wrong is that you judge other people by those standards. Even the most militant atheist who denies the existence of objective moral values gets angry and offended when someone steals from him ... or cuts in line in front of him ... or lies to him ... or breaks a promise. "He shouldn't do that!" is the reaction. "He should know better!" Suddenly they react as if there are objective moral values "everyone should know." And, of course, there are.

No matter what religious background people have, no matter if they are agnostics or atheists, one thing you can know: We all know right from wrong. We all know we should tell the truth ... deal honestly with others ... recognize other people's property ... respect our parents and other legitimate authorities ... be loyal and faithful to our friends ... keep our word. We all know we should not lie, steal, or cheat. We all know we should not harm innocent or vulnerable people. I am reminded of what the ancient sage Confucius said:

> Without money, man cannot survive. Without knowing right from wrong, man cannot be a human being.

Are there difficult ethical decisions to make in this messy world? Of course. Sometimes there are no good choices, and we must select the least bad of several undesirable options. But more often than not, people know the right thing to do.

The difference between people is not that some people know right from wrong and others don't. The difference is that some people have thought through what they believe and have committed themselves to the pursuit of right … and others haven't. The latter are people who have suppressed their knowledge of right and wrong and have chosen to do what feels right at the moment or advances them toward things they want. It is possible to calcify your conscience, so you don't feel anything when you do wrong, but there's a heavy price to pay for it in loss of authentic humanity.

You must make your own choice, but only those who take Principle Convictions seriously can grow into the best kind of leaders and succeed over time.

3. Philosophical Convictions: Your judgment of what matters most to you

Unlike Principle Convictions which apply to all people, Philosophical Convictions are highly personal. They are your judgments of how you want to devote your time and energies.

In the coaching process I use, we do an exercise where clients rank in order their strongest motivating values. There are no right or wrong answers because everyone has the freedom to work these things out for themselves. It is part of our "unalienable right" to "life, liberty, and the pursuit of happiness" asserted in the Declaration of Independence.

One person lists "Career Advancement" at the top, followed by "Achievement" and "Financial Security." Another says "Spirituality" is most important, followed by "Family Balance" and "Contribution to Society." Each is completely free to make their choice, and no one can say another person is wrong, but you can easily see that how someone answers will shape their attitudes and actions. The most important thing is knowing what is most important to you, and making sure your values harmonize with your real-life commitments.

You can see there's a lot to think about. I want to emphasize that, in order to be of value, these things must be predetermined. They need to be in place beforehand, or it will be too late for effective leadership or to withstand the pressures of the moment.

For example, when I received my first opportunity to be the primary leader of an organization, I had already spent ten years thinking through what I believed and determining my philosophy, values, and purposes. Therefore, even during the interview process I could say, "Here's what I believe ... These are my objectives ... This is my philosophy, how I intend to go about it ... These are my values ... These are my nonnegotiables." If people ask you as a new leader what you stand for, and your reply is, "Um ... uh ... let me get back to you on that," you are simply not prepared to lead.

Only you can determine what you believe. I will tell you that by knowing what you believe and being able to *articulate it clearly*, you will stand out in a world where genuine convictions are few and far between. You will be one of those who sets himself on fire and wins followers who are attracted by the light and heat.

Knowing what *not* to change

Some people think that convictions are a hindrance; that holding unchanging beliefs and philosophies is incompatible with the ability to respond to the torrent of change we experience in the world. The truth is exactly the opposite.

Mere change is not the same as progress. You can only call a change progress if you are advancing toward a desired goal. You can change your way to failure through not understanding *why* you are making those changes. Think of the times a company has changed a product to "improve" it, only to damage their brand. In the 1960s, Ford created the wildly-popular Mustang. After a few years of success, they started playing with it. Their "improvements" caused the Mustang to lose its identity and sales dropped. Ford President Lee Iacocca said at the time, "The Mustang market never left us, we left it." Then there was Coca-Cola in the 1980s who decided the best-selling soft drink in the world and one of the most powerful brands ever created needed improving. "New Coke" was a notorious corporate disaster.

In a world of constant change, it is critically important to know what *not* to change. Your nonnegotiable core of identity, values, and philosophies gives you a solid base from which you can question everything else. This is the way to avoid sacred cows from developing, which go on to hinder decision-making.

You still develop plans and strategies, of course, but when you have a core of unchanging convictions those plans and strategies serve *you* instead of you being bound to serve *them*. Executive Harry Quadracci described leadership of a company this way:

> Using plans and budgets is like firing a cannonball. It's fine if you're shooting at a castle. But markets today are moving targets. The only way to hit them is to launch your business like a cruise missile: You fire it in the general direction of your objective. Then its own information systems adjust its course as it draws near.[2]

The metaphor of information systems adjusting your course represents your values, convictions, and philosophies by which you have built your culture or subculture. When your team shares those qualities, you can act as one according to the needs of the present while remaining anchored.

Finally, knowing which commitments are nonnegotiable makes it *safe* to compromise and adapt. Both are rooted in the ground, but there is a reason a palm tree can withstand a hurricane and an oak tree will not. The palm bends in the fierce winds, while the oak holds firm rigidly until it snaps. The roots represent your unchanging convictions. Anything else can be challenged, questioned, and changed when you judge it wise to do so.

What are *you* committed to?

Marshmallow leaders are quite happy to define values *other people* are supposed to live up to. I suppose that's how so many organizations have ended up with corporate values that are published, but not on the radar screens of the leaders themselves. They are for the employees, while executives operate under different rules.

If you want to be an effective leader, you can't give in to that superficial tendency. *Any* values you want to promote through the ranks must apply to you and all other leaders as well. In fact, you must do more than salute them. You must be a raging carrier of the values. As Don Ostroff, one of my early mentors, used to say, "If you want your people to bleed, you're going to have to hemorrhage."

You promote the values you believe, first and foremost, by living them. Just as important are your attitudes toward personal growth and learning. In my firm opinion and experience, there is no more important indicator of someone's leadership potential than teachability. My friend and fellow Sherpa coach Steve Laswell writes (emphasis his):

> No question, *one of the best ways* top executives can get their leaders to improve is *to work on improving themselves*. Leading by example can mean a lot more than leading by public-relations hype.

Steve goes on to issue a warning (emphasis mine):

> Unfortunately, CEO arrogance can have the opposite effect. When the boss acts like a little god and tells *everyone else* THEY need to improve, that behavior can be copied at every level of management. *Every level then points out how the level below it needs to change.* The result: No one gets better.[3]

This kind of hypocrisy is deadly. How leaders behave trumps any words they say. The greater the gap between rhetoric and reality, the more cynical and dysfunctional the organization.

That means that if you genuinely want to build a team or organization around stated values, it must be insisted upon from the start that you and every other leader involved are committing yourselves to the same things you are teaching. You agree to hold each other accountable and agree to remain open to question and correction from any member of the organization no matter where he or she ranks in the hierarchy.

Horace Porter was the personal secretary of Ulysses S. Grant during the Civil War. Writing of his experiences years later, he mentions an incident that occurred during the siege of Petersburg:

> The day the wharf was completed and planked over the general took a stroll along it, his hands thrust in his trouser pockets and a lighted cigar in his mouth. . . . and had not gone far when a sentinel called out: "It's against orders to come on the wharf with a lighted cigar." The general at once took his Havana out of his mouth and threw it into the river, saying, "I don't like to lose my smoke, but the sentinel's right. He evidently isn't going to let me disobey my own orders."[4]

Grant did right. You must declare and defend the principle that being challenged according to the values is a good thing and that it is desired and welcomed. As Marshall Goldsmith commented, "Encouraging upward challenge is a key to maintaining corporate integrity." Since any of us individually, as well as teams, can stray, it is often the lone, small voice of one person that keeps a group from going wrong together. The freedom to hold leaders accountable is one of the best protections for an organization.

Bones are most attractive on the inside

I am obviously a fervent promoter of developing a firm backbone of conviction, but let me add a word of caution. Recall that there are two kinds of skeletons in the animal world: Exoskeletons, where animals wear their bones on the outside, and endoskeletons, where animals wear their bones on the inside.

Question: Which would you rather hug?

No doubt about it. A hug from a human being with strong bones on the inside covered with warm, soft flesh on the outside beats a creature with a hard, cold exoskeleton any day. How would you like a hug from a six-foot lobster?

People's convictions can metaphorically fit either category. There are many who wear their convictions on the outside. They are obnoxious, hard, and unfeeling. They seem to truly believe what they're saying (they are definitely not of the marshmallow type), but they make their convictions unappealing. Plus, they exhibit a common effect of having an exoskeleton, which is stunted personal growth. We've all known people like this, whether their beliefs were in the category of religion, politics, or business. They embody Churchill's definition of a fanatic: "One who can't change his mind and won't change the subject." If you don't buy what they're selling, they only communicate rejection, disdain, and combativeness. They are offering you a hug from a six-foot lobster, and you want no part of it.

There are other people whose convictions are just as firm and unyielding, but who incarnate those beliefs through a warm, attractive humanity. They know what they believe, but they are understanding and compassionate with human frailty. They are kind, merciful, and forgiving. Their decency, gratitude, and consistency make them attractive, and lend credence to the sincerity of their convictions, even if you don't share them all. Their credibility rises the more you get to know them.

These are the people capable of being effective leaders and winning fiercely loyal followers.

So develop your convictions, and let them be as firm and unyielding as you think necessary. Just don't forget to clothe them in gracious, attractive humanity. After all, you are also an imperfect human being at best in the process of learning and growing yourself.

Leading Insights

Part II: Proposition 4
The Backbone of Leadership Is *Conviction*

- In a world of hypocrisy, compromises, and sham, people are attracted to a man or woman who believes something: Deep commitment to values, philosophies, or truths that are unchanging and nonnegotiable.

- The real test: Will you hold to what you say you believe even if doing so costs you something?

- The best and most enduring leaders possess convictions, the bones of character.

- By knowing what you believe and being able to articulate it clearly, you will stand out in a world where genuine convictions are few and far between.

- Any values you want to promote through the ranks must apply to you and all other leaders as well.

- Develop your convictions, but clothe them in gracious, attractive humanity.

Leadership Proposition 5
The *Power* of Leadership Is the *Ability to Define Reality*

All leaders of organizations and teams are interested in unity, that essential quality that marks a group coordinating and cooperating with each other to attain success.

Everybody wants it. Few understand where unity comes from or how to achieve it.

Unity doesn't come about by chance. You don't produce unity by listing it as a value. You also don't get unity by talking about "unity." In fact, leaders who talk a lot about unity usually end up stimulating more disunity and finger-pointing because it's always someone else who is the problem: "If only he/she/they would straighten up, we could be unified!"

To arrive at the true answer, we must come to grips with this fact: You can't create unity directly ... only *indirectly*.

Unity is a result

Unity comes about in the same way that a symphony orchestra with over a hundred individual instruments tunes together. If you attend a concert, you'll notice that the musicians do not tune to each other. You don't see this violin being tuned to the next violin, to the viola, to the cello, to the clarinet, to the French horn, etc. It would take forever, for one thing. By the time they had gotten several instruments in tune, the first ones would have lost their tuning. Besides, you would also have the problem of progressive generations being farther away from the original, just as each photocopy of a photocopy loses some of its clarity.

Do you know what they actually do? The concertmaster signals the oboist to play an "A" and everyone tunes to that note. Since they are all tuning to the same standard, *they are automatically tuned to one another.* You develop unity in

99

an organization or team exactly the same way. Unity is a by-product of people "tuning" to a *common standard.*

That's the essence of leading: Setting the standard you want people to tune their minds to and persuading them to accept it and act accordingly. This principle is what executive and author Max De Pree had in mind when he said, "The first responsibility of a leader is to define reality."[1]

The power of leadership

In any situation, large or small, there will be conflicting definitions of reality. People's disagreements can be about the biggest questions:

- "Who are we? What are our core beliefs?"
- "What is our objective?"
- "What constitutes success?"
- "Who do we serve?"
- "What behaviors are acceptable and unacceptable?"

Or people's disagreements can be about a current problem or crisis:

- "This is terrible! We're doomed!"
- "This is their fault!"
- "Our executives are idiots! They don't know what they're doing!"
- "This is a difficult challenge, but we can get through this if we put our heads together and get after it. In fact, we might even be able to use this to our advantage. Here's what I'm thinking ..."

Whichever definition of reality takes hold as the dominant view of the group, it will determine everything that follows. Whoever is able to state his or her definition of reality in a situation and win the acceptance of others in the group is the one who emerges as the leader, no matter if they hold a title and authority or not.

That's why I assert Leadership Proposition 5: **The *Power* of Leadership Is the *Ability to Define Reality*.** It is the leader's ability to sound the key note to which others tune.

The unspoken question on followers' minds

In any pressure situation, especially in a crisis, people look to their leader. There is always a question on their minds, usually unspoken. Do you know what it is? They are asking, "How should we think about this?" They will take their cue and proceed based on the definition of reality their leader presents. Defining reality means *teaching people how to think about things.*

As a simple illustration, let's say you are managing an office facing a deadline when the flu takes out three of your people. What might your remaining team members be thinking?

"This week is going to suck!"

"We'll never get this done!"

"Woe is me! Everything bad always happens to us!"

Eventually, all their eyes turn to you. They are asking that unspoken question. How will you define reality?

Your message must be both realistic and confident: "We are short some key people, and there's nothing we can do about that. Things will get chaotic around here this week. We can expect lots of pressures, lots of demands, and some long hours." [= realism] "But we've done it before. We can do it again. We have a great team. If we all put on the right attitude and work together, we can stay on top of this and come out successful." [= confidence] "Meanwhile, I'll be working to get us some temporary help."

When leaders define reality with realism and confidence in a persuasive way, people tend to start nodding and thinking, "We can do this," and they rise to the occasion.

Please note: *Defining reality is NOT the same thing as its bastardized cousin, "spin."* Spin is about manipulating people with dishonest methods of persuasion. It is about using language to *deny* and *distort* reality rather than framing it truly in an optimistic problem-solving manner. Spin is what we hear on a daily basis during the election season, or when corporate or government leaders are caught lying or in a scandal.

Many of the public spin attempts I hear remind me of an outrageous scene in the movie *Naked Gun*. The villain drives into a gasoline truck that propels him onto a missile that runs into a fireworks factory. As a crowd of awed spectators are drawn to the fireworks and explosions, Leslie Nielson as Lt. Frank Drebin stands directly in front of the scene waving his arms and shouting, "There's nothing to see here! Everyone disperse! Nothing to see here!"

Trying to use spin to deny obvious reality can leave you looking ridiculous. It is not what effective leaders do, and it is not the same as defining reality.

The goal: Likeminded people

People behave alike when they think alike. You don't hear the word used much these days, but my favorite term for what you're after is "likemindedness."

It doesn't matter what kind of organization or team you lead, whether it's a large corporation or a small office. Likemindedness expresses exactly what you want to develop as a leader: A team that thinks alike. A team that *thinks alike* will *act* alike, just as the musicians playing many different instruments can play a single piece.

Creating likemindedness is one of the secrets of developing a high-functioning team with members who can act on their own reliably and safely. You can trust their behaviors and decision-making when they are out of your sight because you and they have worked hard at getting your minds together. When people have bought into your definition of reality, they will behave in a predictable manner.

This view does not mean conformity in personality, temperament, or opinions. This principle is not about imposing sameness on people. In fact, you want diversity in individual strengths and perspectives, because they make for a stronger team. I am talking about a common commitment to the same philosophy, purposes, and values. The result of this common commitment is genuine and strong unity, a likemindedness that allows the organization or team to move in concert toward common objectives and goals.

The requirement: Sufficient Leadership Effect

Your power to define reality is the result of all the leadership qualities we have examined so far.

Your clarity and confidence in defining and communicating the key note come from your convictions — those principles, philosophies, and values you genuinely and deeply believe.

Your attitude of optimism inspires others to accept your view that the future can be better if they buy into your message.

Finally, people's willingness to hear you and take your message seriously rests on the foundation of your total Leadership Effect, the credibility you have earned through your professional competence and personal conduct.

Remember, the most important thing is not your desire to lead, but your diligence in preparing to lead. This moment of opportunity, challenge, or crisis is when the bill comes due. If you have properly prepared, you are likely to be successful as a leader. If you haven't, there's not much chance you'll find people disposed to following you.

A sharply-defined purpose

People ask, "What is our purpose?" Without clarity and unity about purpose, people will go in different directions according to their own view of priorities. Statements of mission, vision, and values are *supposed* to provide the basis for unity, but we all know they seldom do. They are too often just nice words on a poster or plaque, and they are typically ponderous and badly written.

In *Dilbert*, Scott Adams defined a mission statement as:

A long awkward sentence that demonstrates management's inability to think clearly.[2]

He gave this example:

We enhance stockholder value through strategic business initiatives by empowered employees working in new team paradigms.[3]

How inspiring.

Effective leaders don't leave the purpose of their organization or team up for grabs. They present and defend a sharply-defined statement of "the main thing." Here are some examples from different spheres:

Henry Ford: To "build a motor car for the great multitude ... so low in price that no man making a good salary will be unable to own one."

John F. Kennedy: "... this Nation should commit itself to achieving the goal, before this decade is out, of landing a man on the moon and returning him safely to earth."

General Electric: "Become #1 or #2 in every market we serve and revolutionize this company to have the speed and agility of a small enterprise."

Frances Hesselbein [the Girl Scouts]: "We are here for only one reason: to help girls and young women reach their highest potential."

Red Cross: "to provide compassionate care to those in need ... preventing and relieving suffering, here at home and around the world."

Mary Kay: "To give unlimited opportunity to women."

Walmart: "Saving people money so they can live better."

Some of these are from the past and not necessarily the current stated purposes of those organizations, but they illustrate my point. Someone might be uninterested or disagree with them, but no one can misunderstand them. All are sharp and clear definitions of purpose. As such they provide the North Star to which people can align their thinking and efforts.

Likemindedness through a deliberately constructed culture

Defined, culture is "the set of shared attitudes, values, goals, and practices that characterizes an institution or organization." *Every group has a culture.* It's not *If?* It's *What kind?* Where cultures differ is whether they are:

- ***Designed or accidental***
  They can be intelligently and deliberately developed and maintained, like a building that grows from a blueprint, or they can be formed like a sand dune, shaped by whatever winds are blowing.

- ***Based on principles or personalities***
  Cultures can be built according to unchanging values, which apply to every person, or cultures can take the shape of their most dominant, strong-willed personalities and then run according to the current moods of those persons.

- ***Healthy or unhealthy***
  A culture can be mature and honest in communication, affirming and respectful of individuals, and stimulating and motivating, resulting in positive performance, or it can be immature and manipulative, even abusive. An unhealthy culture can be characterized by demotivating pressures in the effort to generate performance, proving in the long run to be counterproductive.

In a business setting, culture applies on the very large scale, such as a company of thousands of employees, or on the very small scale, such as an office with only a handful of workers. Within the culture of a large company are also many subcultures. Each department, site, or office has its own version, which may or may not be in character with the whole.

You should be interested in your group's culture, no matter how large or small it is because a group's culture is the most reliable indicator of future performance. Howard H. Stevenson of the Harvard School of Business said:

> Great leaders build strong cultures. They get people to agree on a model of the world.[4]

In my experience, the critical importance of culture is not always recognized. A group's culture forms the entire background of the human behavior that goes on within it. It's the social atmosphere. It's the air you breathe as you do your work. Like the Earth's atmosphere, it can be healthy or toxic. Only foolish organizational leaders ignore culture, believing that it's all about coming up with a brilliant strategy. As Peter Drucker said, "Culture eats strategy for breakfast."

In my firm opinion, one of the prime responsibilities of any leader is the development and maintenance of a healthy values- and performance-based culture. Regardless of the size of the sphere, the group's culture must be a daily object of concern. It's a form of "climate control," like checking and adjusting a team's thermostat.

Lewis V. Gerstner, Jr., who led the resurgence of IBM in the 1990s concluded:

> I came to see, in my time at IBM, that culture isn't just one aspect of the game — it *IS* the game.[5]

I totally concur. Effective leaders don't leave culture to chance. They work at culture definition and development until purposes, values, and philosophies are infused into the corporate DNA of their people, shaping what they think, say, and do.

How do they do it? How can you get those characteristics into people's DNA?

The process for developing a culture

The process for developing a culture is simple to understand, though a definite leadership challenge to accomplish. This is my way of explaining it:

1. **DEFINE**
2. **SHAPE**
3. **ALIGN**

Begin by **defining** your purpose and values. Values, remember, cannot be words you "choose"; you *discover* them by looking within and identifying what you *already really believe*. You must believe them, or you'll never have the tenacity to pursue them over the long haul. I think this is the reason so many organizations have values statements that makes little difference in actual behavior. Leaders "picked" them because they sounded good, but didn't do the hard work of digging in and identifying what they are willing to commit themselves to in practice. These statements must be convictions. Otherwise, you have marshmallow values.

The second step is to **shape** your purpose statement and values to be *memorable* and *easily understood*. You want your people to be able to repeat them with ease. The best values statements usually include no more than four points, because the average person cannot remember more than that without effort. There are exceptions to this general rule, but you'll find that those organizations who successfully practice more than four have designed specific processes to promote and reinforce them.

Third, commit to the never-ending process of **aligning** your group's efforts and behaviors according to the statements. This is the real battle. In the heat of everyday pressures, will you insist that attitudes, actions, and processes conform to those values to which you are committed? Here is where you discover the truth above, which is that you must genuinely hold the values as convictions, or they will go by the wayside when you encounter temptation or resistance.

I frankly believe that if an organization is not prepared to follow through with long-term action, they are better off not having stated values at all. Values and principles that are contradicted by leaders' attitudes, behaviors, and decision-making spread cynicism throughout the ranks, which functions like a cultural poison. No one is fooled, and hypocrisy spreads.

A standard principle in civil law is, "Where there is no law, there is no violation." In other words, you must have a defined standard before you can hold people accountable to it. Besides giving a basis for accountability, defining and promoting your values frees you from the charge of playing favorites. If everyone is expected to live up to a value, then it isn't "personal" when you call someone to align with it. Likemindedness according to core values is what you require from *everyone*, including yourself.

Examples of defined cultures

The most successful organizations in the world show the power of a culture built by design, where leaders have defined their core values and aligned people's attitudes, behaviors, and efforts accordingly.

Southwest Airlines

One of my favorite positive examples over the years has been Dallas-based Southwest Airlines. It has been a competitor in the world of air travel since the late 1960s and one of the most consistently profitable. Co-founder and long-time CEO Herb Kelleher was the leading proponent of one of the most unique and quirky corporate cultures around. Ask any Southwest employee, from the pilots to the mechanical crew to the executives, what the Southwest values are, and you'll get a quick answer:

- Warrior Spirit
- Servant's Heart
- Fun-LUVing Attitude

Going back to their days as a small regional carrier, Southwest's "Warrior Spirit" expressed their aggressive attitude: "Look out, American and Delta. We're coming against the big boys!" "Servant's Heart" means they seek to genuinely care for employees inside and their customers outside. "Fun-LUVing Attitude" says, "We may take our work very seriously, but we refuse to take ourselves seriously. We intend to have fun doing what we love." Each one of the three values is spelled out in bullet points, so their meaning will be crystal-clear.

A story related in a periodical underscores Southwest's commitment to their culture. A highly-recommended pilot interviewed with them. One of their executives commented, "He was the most competent-looking person we've ever seen on paper." The pilot received rave reviews from Southwest pilots on the panel that interviewed him, but that pilot was not hired. Why? "He was rude to the reservations agent when he booked a flight to come to the interview. He wasn't polite to the coordinator who set up the interview. He was rude to the receptionist when he came in for the interview." When the pilot later asked why he had been rejected, he was told the reasons loud and clear. The executive commented, "He treated the people most important to us poorly."[6] That's a company that takes its stated values seriously.

Herb Kelleher was the leading cheerleader and example of these values. He embodied them, making sure that they were not only consistently promoted and lived, but — just as important — rewarded. Though a savvy businessman and a tough, shrewd negotiator, he considered cultural development and protection a prime responsibility, and would do practically anything to promote them. In pursuit of a "Fun-LUVing Attitude," for example, you might find him serving pizza or doughnuts in a chicken suit or a cocktail dress, participating as Elvis in a surprise pie-throwing contest, or involved in a host of bizarre activities.

Kelleher was a leader willing to set himself on fire. People did come from miles around to see him burn. That fire was fueled by genuine beliefs that did not waver in hard times or flap in the wind.

Ritz-Carlton Hotels

Ritz-Carlton has set the standard for exceptional customer service for decades, and that's no accident. Ritz-Carlton has defined and deliberately institutionalized their commitments and values and has built a culture around them.

In an age when customer service is basically mediocre everywhere you go, how does this large international company maintain a culture and behaviors that set it apart so dramatically? You can see for yourself by looking up the public document called "The Ritz-Carlton Gold Standards." It defines the cultural DNA that makes the Ritz what it is.

Ritz-Carlton begins defining reality by addressing the fundamental questions of human experience, those that revolve around identity, meaning, and purpose: "Who am I?" "Why am I here?" "What gives meaning and purpose to my actions?" The motto for all Ritz-Carlton employees reads, "We are Ladies and Gentlemen serving Ladies and Gentlemen."

I absolutely love this motto. Do you see the ramifications of it? One of the reasons people resist serving others is the mistaken notion that serving is somehow demeaning: "If I serve someone else, it must mean I'm not as good as they are." The RC Motto turns this totally around. "Who am I? I am a Lady" or "a Gentleman." "What do I do? I serve Ladies and Gentlemen." There is dignity, value, and purpose in this self-concept, and it frees people to serve guests happily without any feelings of being demeaned or "unworthy."

If you read the whole page (well worth your time), you'll notice that the RC standards are all about *active* service, unlike the mediocre passive service you find in the average retail store: A clerk mumbling, "If you need anything, let me know." RC employees are all about looking, watching, thinking, and seeking to be of service. It's figuring out how to help before the guest asks, maybe before she has become aware of it herself. Experience certainly helps in anticipating needs, but it has to begin with a servant's attitude, or all the experience in the world is of little use. Excellent customer service is always intentional and active.

A deliberate process to build culture

The Ritz-Carlton Gold Standards are quite long. By my count, there are more than 20 individual points, so they are an exception to my general rule of having only three or four core values. The only way to inject more than 20 ideas into people's minds is through a deliberate process. That is exactly how they do it, according to my research.

Every work team begins the day with a huddle, including a ten-minute discussion of one of the points from the Gold Standards. You might ask, "How much can ten minutes accomplish?" I answer, "It's not the ten minutes. It's the *every day* that does it." In the course of a year, each employee will discuss every point on the list around 15 times. The constant reinforcement drips, drips, drips into people's thinking, and thinking drives behavior. The result is a defined culture that produces excellent customer service.

Never waste a meeting

That's why one of my regular themes in coaching leaders is to promote the philosophy: "Never waste a meeting." Here's what I mean: Whatever reason you might have for a meeting, formal or informal, take it as an opportunity to apply some leadership and to build your culture. You might be meeting for an hour to discuss selling widgets, yes, but anytime you have a captive audience, use 5-10 minutes of it to raise people's sights. Talk about your vision for your group … share some recent example where a key value came into play … discuss what one of your core values means to you … ask what a core value means to them, and hold a discussion.

You cannot build a culture through a single ninety-minute speech. You build it by drip, drip, dripping it into people's minds and aligning actions until they adopt it as their own.

Are Southwest Airlines and Ritz-Carlton perfect? Of course not. You can find disgruntled individuals and examples of where they fall short, just as in every other company because they are made up of ordinary human beings. If they fail to continue the processes by which they have built their cultures, they will decline. Cultures are fragile and must be continuously reinforced.

As a leadership developer and executive coach, I have worked in many organizations, and I have yet to find a perfect one. I will say, however, that some of them are much better than others, and it is not by accident. Let me encourage you: If you make an honest effort over time to identify and faithfully practice the values you believe, your organization or team will be well above average. How do I know that? Because so few organizations even make the effort.

If you concentrate on developing organizational health, the rest seems to take care of itself and smooths over people's imperfections. You develop organizational health through defining, shaping, and aligning according to your genuine values.

What do you want?

Defining reality begins in your own mind, in knowing what you want as an outcome. How do you want the people of your organization or team to answer these questions?

On organizational focus:
- What is our purpose
- Who are we
- Who are our customers
- How do we define success
- What will we measure

On cultural values:
- What are our values
- What behaviors are acceptable and unacceptable
- What qualities matter the most to us

That's just the beginning. Defining your answers to these questions, shaping them to be clear and memorable, and then aligning people to them is how you build a healthy culture of likeminded people. The result will be genuine unity.

Let me warn you: It's hard work. Why? Because thinking is hard work, which is the reason most people try to avoid it.

You can't afford to avoid this kind of thinking if you want to be an effective leader. Your power as a leader is wrapped up in your ability to define reality for your followers.

Leading Insights

Part II: Proposition 5
The Power of Leadership Is the
Ability to Define Reality

- You cannot create unity directly. Unity is a by-product of people's commitment to a common standard.

- The first requirement of a leader is to define reality: Teaching people how to think about things.

- Effective leaders define and relentlessly promote a sharp definition of purpose.

- The process for building a culture by design:
  1. Define
  2. Shape
  3. Align

- Never waste a meeting. Any time you have a captive audience, use 5-10 minutes to build your culture and values.

Leadership Proposition 6
The *Character* of Leadership Is *Authenticity*

T he leadership credibility you earn through your professional competence (knowledge and skills) and your personal conduct (behaviors) is the single most important factor that influences people to be willing to follow you. Your total Leadership Effect is the result.

This is the point where I must warn you of its vulnerability and weakness.

Your leadership credibility is only the starting point. It is what induces people to follow you, but it is *not* a once-and-done issue.

Don't expect to fool anyone

You know this upon a little reflection. How many leaders have you known personally or from a distance through history or the news, who started out with flying colors only to flame out in failure? They projected strength, confidence, and competence. They appeared to be effective leaders, and people bought into them. Eventually, though, their lack of substance was exposed, and they failed.

Why were people taken in? It's simple. The qualities that initially encourage credibility *are easy to counterfeit*. With people's natural tendencies to be attracted to the Conventional Model of a leader, it's fairly simple for a would-be leader with sufficient emotional intelligence to figure out what the ingredients are and project those qualities.

That is, it's fairly simple for *a while*. Eventually, reality is exposed. Henry B. Thayer, who led AT&T back in the 1920s, said this:

> It is easy to fool yourself. It is possible to fool the people you work for. It is more difficult to fool the people you work with. But it is impossible to fool the people who work under you.[1]

That's why I say to any aspiring leader, "Don't count on fooling anyone. The people who work around you every day will eventually know you backwards and forwards if they don't already. If you're not real, believe me, they will know it."

The ancient Romans had a proverb: "Truth is the daughter of time." Over time, the truth comes out. If you want to succeed as a leader long-term, you should take that proverb to heart and choose to pursue Leadership Proposition 6: **The *Character* of Leadership Is *Authenticity*.**

How to destroy credibility

Derek was intelligent, energetic, and hard working. A former consultant, he was gifted at sounding like he knew what he was talking about on most any subject. He was socially smooth and had a way of making people like him quickly. He sold his way into a significant corporate position, but he eventually failed and was terminated by his superiors. What happened?

Derek wasn't authentic. That fact was picked up on by the people who worked around him. Interestingly, the order in which they figured him out followed the observations above by Henry B. Thayer. It took only a few weeks for his subordinates to catch on that he couldn't be trusted. It took a few months for his peers in other departments to figure out that he wasn't what he seemed to be. It took a couple of years for his superiors to become disenchanted with Derek and to decide they could dispense with his services.

Here is a sample of the behaviors that sank his ship.

Revealing a two-faced way of dealing with people. At a lunch with several members of his team, Derek lavishly praised Mary's contribution to a recent project. She "did great," and he "really appreciated" her effort. Those comments were in context with everything he had ever said to Mary. Later that afternoon, Derek confided to Martha (Mary's peer): "I've decided that Mary's not going to make it. She just doesn't have the skills I need. I'm planning to dump her after the New Year." Martha didn't feel complimented by receiving that inside knowledge. It created distrust and insecurity.

Betraying the confidence of absent parties. Similar to the above behavior, Derek was all charm when a member of another department or a superior came in for a conversation. He displayed every appearance of an eager and positive team member in their presence. But after that person left, the gloves came off. "I can't imagine how that man became a VP," he said to all within earshot. "He's totally incompetent. You wouldn't believe the stupid things he says in our senior team meetings." Once again, being included in the intimacy of his real opinions did not make his subordinates feel they were "in the know." Any intelligent person would think, "If Derek talks about *Vice Presidents* behind their backs, what does he say about *me* when *I'm* not present?" More trust was destroyed.

Derek assumed he was winning people into his confidence by these practices, but he wasn't. He was also foolish enough to believe that the things he said to his team would remain private. Of course, they didn't. Word mysteriously got back to the people he had bad-mouthed in their absence, and those opinions were not forgotten. Personal charm not only doesn't erase them, but the syrupy friendliness Derek exhibited in person just made it worse.

Throwing other people under the bus to protect himself. On the leadership level, Derek's one inviolate value was self-preservation. Peers and others above him learned over months that if Derek ever felt exposed, it was always the fault of someone else or of another department. It caused other powerful leaders to begin raising their guard around him. Whatever credibility he had been granted because of his positive first impressions eroded away steadily until there was none left. Ultimately, it was good-bye.

Authenticity defined

Clarification is needed at this point because I commonly find confusion over the meaning of authenticity, especially as it relates to transparency. These concepts are often mingled or considered interchangeable, but that is a great mistake.

Let me share my working definition of each.

Transparency means "you can see everything." Like the view through a clean window pane, nothing is hidden. You can see everything, and what you see is what you get.

Authenticity means "what you see is real." There's no promise that you can see everything, but you can be confident that what you see is true. It's not fake, misleading, or deceptive. It's solid, dependable.

Both are appropriate in their place. There are organizational categories where transparency is exactly right and necessary. Examples include ethical standards, policies, financial procedures, and reporting. But, there are certain leadership applications where I believe practicing complete transparency is a huge mistake — especially where you are revealing *everything you think and feel.*

I typically grant people the benefit of the doubt and assume the best until they prove otherwise. I assume that you are a good man or woman who wants to be an honest, hard-working, productive, and improving professional. I assume you want to learn more about leadership because you want to help make things **BETTER**.

Let's also be honest. We all have some bad habits, negative traits, and — especially damaging in a leadership role — doubts and fears. The transparent display of these characteristics can undermine or totally destroy your ability to lead.

What you reveal publicly

As a leader, your attitudes are more contagious than a flu virus, and therefore, what you reveal in public must be by careful calculation. If you are feeling negative and discouraged and show it transparently, you can create a storm of negativity and discouragement throughout an entire organization.

When you get down to it, your followers don't want to know about all your weaknesses, fears, and doubts. Knowing those things increases their doubts, fears, and uncertainties. In the most stressful or fearful times, people would rather retain some illusions for comfort's sake. It helps them keep going.

I have written previously about Winston Churchill as an example of optimistic leadership under great pressure. What I didn't share at the time was that Churchill struggled terribly with periods of deep depression. He called it "the Black Dog." However, knowing his role, Churchill kept those experiences private, so he could offer public leadership. Abraham Lincoln was another famous leader, among many examples, who experienced bouts of despondency and depression, but projected confidence and courage in public. Imagine the havoc those leaders would have created had they openly shared with the public what they felt during those periods of depression.

Simply put, as a leader you cannot afford to practice complete transparency, *especially* in regard to your inner thoughts and feelings. If you violate this principle, you can quickly undermine everything you are trying to accomplish as a leader. In other words, be *aware* and wise in what you say and do. Your job is to impart optimism about your eventual success. Be authentic — real, dependable, and optimistic — and you'll build your followers' confidence.

All of us deal with pressure from a variety of fronts. Anyone who has functioned as a leader for several years has had to do so while privately carrying emotional burdens. It could be a difficult marriage, a special needs child, troublesome teenagers, health worries, or extended family problems. Leaders don't get an exemption from these life issues. They are, however, expected to continue functioning as if they didn't exist. One of the burdens of leadership is the necessity to put personal concerns aside mentally in order to be fully "on duty" in your role. It requires strength, maturity, and discipline to do so.

I believe authenticity was what Frances Hesselbein was pointing toward in comments I quoted in the first chapter:

> The leader beyond the millennium will not be the leader who has learned the lessons of *how to do it* ... The leader of today and for the future will be focused on how to *BE* — how to develop quality, character, mind-set, values, principles, and courage.[2]

Leadership is not just about *doing*, it's about authentically *being* who you are.

Organizational leaders face the difficult balance of functioning with authority while cultivating positive relationships. Authenticity enables you to be yourself while at the same time maintaining proper professional boundaries with subordinates and others.

Remember the dark side of human nature

Again, let me reiterate my personal philosophy of assuming good will on the part of others. I find most people prove worthy of that assumption, but don't ever forget what kind of world we live in. This world is not a safe place. Everyone is not to be trusted. There are dishonest and unethical people out there, especially anywhere you find a concentration of power and wealth — like the world of business for instance.

It is not safe to be completely transparent in this world. Knowledge is power, and any information you give away can be used against you by unscrupulous persons. How can we sort this out? I believe authenticity is the answer.

There have been times in my career I came to realize I was dealing with an untrustworthy person. I didn't want to betray my own value system of how to treat others properly, but I also didn't want to become vulnerable to someone I didn't trust. Keep in mind my working definition of authenticity: "What you see is real." I chose to continue being normally friendly, courteous, respectful, and professional in my behavior toward him or her, but I also made the decision to hold back personal information. I kept my mouth shut regarding any potentially controversial opinions. I didn't speak in their presence about my personal life or history. I *especially* made sure not to make negative comments about any absent persons, knowing anything I said would be repeated.

Authenticity means you can be yourself and reveal as much of yourself as you please, while withholding as much sensitive information as you judge necessary for your own protection. You can be real without promising to reveal absolutely everything.

Having issued these warnings, I want to offer one more subtle distinction. While you can't afford to be completely transparent with all people, you need *some* trusted friends and associates where you can let it all out. As author Ronald Heifetz says, "The lone-warrior model of leadership is heroic suicide."[3] Be sure the persons to whom you choose to unload are both *stable* and *reliable*; that is, they are able to handle what you share without being dragged down by it and are safe to be trusted with your private information. Then guard your tongue in public.

So practice authenticity. While you make no promise that your followers see and know everything about you, you *do* faithfully promise that what they see is *real*.

Authenticity must be modeled

What would you do differently if you knew that your attitudes, speech, behaviors, and habits would be imitated and multiplied by your followers? If you are a leader, guess what? They will be!

That is a sobering fact, and it hits the bulls-eye on the crucial leadership issue of **modeling** — the *example* you set for others.

This statement will be no surprise to those of us who have children, but people will imitate what you *are* more than what you *say*. How many of us have observed with a sting that our children's speech, attitudes, and behavior look disturbingly like our own? How many of us have noticed with surprise that we do things just like Mom or Dad did? That's because modeling is the most powerful source of unconscious learning.

As a leader, you get the kind of behavior you demonstrate. Corporate cultures are ultimately developed by the behaviors of their leaders. On the positive side, this is how a company's culture (or its subcultures, such as departments or offices) can be built in a desirable direction. But always keep in mind that undesirable attitudes, words, and behaviors will also be reproduced down the ranks.

In the remainder of this chapter, I want to share three areas of behavior you can work on that will increase followers' trust in your authenticity as a leader.

1. Integrity in word and deed

Integrity means "wholeness" or "soundness." In engineering, a bridge with integrity will hold up when you drive an eighteen-wheeler over it. According to the dictionary, integrity of character means "the quality or state of being of sound moral principle; uprightness, honesty, and sincerity."

We explored this in Leadership Proposition 4: **The *Backbone* of Leadership Is *Conviction*.** Here in our discussion of authenticity is where the proof will be in the pudding. Anyone can claim to have integrity, but it must be lived out before the watching eyes of followers, and it must be maintained when the heat is on.

Integrity begins with **intellectual honesty**, which means being honest *with yourself.* The person willing to fool him- or herself has gone wrong from the start and cannot lead others with integrity. That failure of integrity will color and shape everything else.

One of my personal convictions is the refusal to engage in manipulation. I believe in straightforward, adult communication with people, not game-playing, passive-aggressive tactics, indirect messages, or playing on emotions such as guilt. I want to be treated like a grownup, and I therefore seek to practice integrity through treating others like grownups.

Another application of integrity is showing loyalty to people in their absence. I try not to speak about absent parties at all, unless there is a specific reason why it's warranted (such as giving advice in a managerial situation, or in coaching an individual how to handle a conflict). Many of us were taught by parents or grandparents, "If you don't have something nice to say about someone, don't say anything at all." That's not a bad rule for the professional environment as well. If I say anything at all about someone who is not present, I seek to say something complimentary. Integrity in this matter will enhance others' view of your authenticity.

You model integrity by keeping your word; if you Do What You Say You Will Do — or short, DWYSYWD. Small slips in this area can cause large losses of trust.

Integrity is about more than ethical decisions, however. You show your integrity also through **consistency**; that is, being predictably "you."

As we have seen throughout this book, there is no particular personality type or temperament you must have to be an effective leader. You will find that followers can adjust to a wide variety of styles in leaders from the loud and boisterous to the quiet and introspective. What followers *cannot* deal well with are leaders who ride a roller-coaster of moods. He or she is up and positive on Monday, down in the dumps Tuesday, strict and demanding on Wednesday, loose and tolerant on Thursday, finally panicked and frantic on Friday.

Your followers will adjust to your personality and style as long as you are consistent in them. Be predictably "you."

You also authentically demonstrate integrity through setting and defending values for your entire organization or team. When you clearly state principles, and then hold people — everyone, including yourself — accountable to them, you prove that your integrity is authentic.

2. Abundant and clear communication

Visit any organization and listen to people long enough to find out what bugs them, and I will venture a bet that one of their chief complaints is lack of communication from leadership. And yet, in those same places, I'll also bet that the leaders *think* they communicate enough. It's almost a universal organizational virus. So accept it as a truism of leadership: Communicate, communicate, and communicate. And when you think you've communicated enough, communicate some more.

About what?

Obviously, we have explored extensively the importance of communicating the core values, philosophies, and principles you believe. I won't belabor that here.

Another area where communication is needed is the issue of **focus**. This is a common failing in organizations, and it has great ramifications. Lewis V. Gerstner, Jr. asserts, "Lack of focus is the most common cause of corporate mediocrity."[4]

People want to know, "What should I focus on? What are the main things? What outcomes are most important to you? What are your expectations of me and of this project?" Without answers to these questions, people don't know where to focus their efforts. Some managers err by issuing lists with 20 or more "priorities." That is less than helpful. I tell them, "*Everything* cannot be a priority. If everything is a priority, *nothing* is a priority." Leaders are responsible for defining to an organization or team what are the main priorities and giving a ranking of them so people can make decisions about their time and activities.

People also want to know, "Where are we going? How does the future look to you? Do you think we'll be successful?" Leaders who fail to communicate adequately in these areas risk the hazard of stimulating people's imaginations into action. Let me warn you: When people don't know what's going on, they will imagine what they think is going on and will almost invariably assume the worst.

Finally, when there really is bad news, never minimize it. Yes, *frame* it appropriately, which is an application of defining reality, but never try to brush it away. First, people can sense when the leader is not being honest. Second, when later the seriousness of the situation becomes clear, people remember, and it can cost you a serious amount of credibility. Third, people can handle bad news when it's given to them straight in adult communication. That gives them the ability to rise to the occasion behind an effective leader and meet the challenge.

The antidote to the anxiety produced by runaway imaginations or negative reality is *clear communication.*

3. Being openly "human"

You demonstrate the authenticity of your character and integrity through the quality of openness. This quality includes being approachable and "human."

People have contradictory feelings about their leaders. They want leaders who seem "better" than they are, which is understandable. After all, they think you know something or have special gifts to take them to a better future. But they don't want leaders who are "too different." They like to see indications that you are human enough to relate to their experience. Here are three ways you can model this quality of being openly "human."

Listen

While your followers require much communication from you, it needs to go both ways. The best leaders are great listeners. Your people have intelligence, talents, and creativity to offer. They see things that could be of great value to your mission, and they see things that need correcting or fixing. A "know-it-all leader" who thinks he or she has all the answers and intelligence necessary makes the grave mistake of ignoring the potential contributions of the people. That's a foolish waste of your greatest resource.

Listening to others' opinions and being open to change does *not* diminish your credibility as a leader. It *raises* your leadership credibility in their eyes.

Have a sense of humor

Being human includes having a sense of humor. Humor can be one of your greatest tools to help people keep or regain perspective and deal with stress. In fact, research has shown that teams that exhibit the most frequent occurrences of laughter are also the highest producing.

You demonstrate authenticity by being able to laugh at yourself. I've known many leaders who had a general sense of humor, but who bristled if they were the object of the laughter. That's a sign of weakness, and it's also a sign that they don't see the truth clearly. Your followers will be keen observers of you and become complete experts in regard to your good *and* *bad* qualities along with any harmless quirks you have. You show stability and maturity by your ability to take gentle teasing in stride. It shows you can be one of the group and increases followers' ability to identify with you.

Show vulnerability

You also model authenticity by showing vulnerability; that is, refusing the temptation to present yourself as "perfect." Number one, you're not. Second, if you could convince people you're beyond faults and failures, you would only increase the distance between you and them, lessoning your Leadership Effect.

It may seem counterintuitive, but there is power in vulnerability. In my leadership development classes through the years, participants have reported that some of the most valuable insights they received were times I departed from the prepared material and told stories, many of which highlighted my failures and mistakes. When you share with people stories about the times you blew it, they can identify with you much better. They see that you, too, have walked a path of development, and that encourages their hope that they can do the same.

We all have weaknesses, and we all make mistakes. Being authentic enough to acknowledge them makes you appear fully three-dimensional and draws people to you. Your credibility with them grows, strengthening your ability to lead.

"Being human" is not a weakness in a leader. It's a strength.

This chapter is chock full of concepts and applications, which may make the pursuit of authenticity seem intimidating. Before I close the chapter, let me simplify the issue.

Leadership Proposition 6: **The *Character* of Leadership Is *Authenticity*** is a reminder that you don't have to fit any particular mold, and certainly not that of the Conventional Model, in order to lead effectively. You can be authentically "you" ... as long as you have the good sense and enough self-awareness to hold back things detrimental to your Leadership Effect. You don't have to ... and *shouldn't* ... reveal *everything*. But you can take steps to ensure that what you share is real. That's being authentic, and that's a demonstration of genuine character.

Leading Insights

Part II: Proposition 6
The *Character* of Leadership Is *Authenticity*

- To succeed as a leader over time, you must be authentic.

- Transparency means "you can see everything." Authenticity means "what you see is real." Authentic appearance is true, solid, and dependable.

- We all have bad habits, negative traits, doubts, and fears. The transparent display of these can undermine or destroy your ability to lead.

- This world is not a safe place. Authenticity means you can be yourself and reveal as much of yourself as you please, while withholding as much sensitive information as you judge necessary for your own protection.

- While you can't afford to be completely transparent with all people, you need some trusted friends and associates where you can let it all out.

- Your leadership credibility is enhanced by comfortably sharing your "human" side.

Leadership Proposition 7
The *Heart* of Leadership Is *Serving*

T he world is full of people who want to become a leader because of the perceived perks that go with the role. You get the ego satisfaction of having people look to you with admiration. You get the tingle of power that you can speak and other people will jump. You feel freedom from accountability and have total discretion to do whatever you want.

Do you believe that? No, those are illusions.

Though that authoritarian illusion is what many people have wanted to attain and have tried to implement, the most effective leaders in the world lead differently. They know the truth of Leadership Proposition 7: **The *Heart* of Leadership Is *Serving*.**

This concept was introduced to the modern business world in 1970 with the publication of *The Servant as Leader* by Robert K. Greenleaf. By the 1980s, the term "servant-leader" was commonplace in the business vocabulary, eventually attaining buzzword status. However, as it typically does, business culture moved on to focus on other fads, and servant leadership became another dated concept "everybody knew about." How many truly understood or practiced it was another matter.

Servant leadership, however, was not created in the 20th century. As a matter of fact, you must go back 2000 years to find its greatest teacher and practitioner: Jesus Christ.

The leader as servant

Jesus' disciples were as normal as any corporate man or woman today in their competitive desire to be Number One. On an occasion when Jesus heard them arguing over which of them was the greatest, he called them together for a corrective conversation. He said:

In the world, kings are tyrants and lord it over their subjects. Holders of power oppress people by their authority. Not so with you. Instead, whoever wants to be the leader must be your servant, and whoever wants the top place must be your slave. Just as I did not come to be served but to serve, and to give my life as a ransom for many.[1]

Jesus' example and teaching on the leader as servant has set the standard for his followers ever since, but this truth is not limited to Christian believers. Any successful organizational leader will tell you that he or she is indeed the servant of all.

Many an ambitious person has hungered to climb the ladder, believing that their rise will mean more and more autonomy, only to discover the opposite. I remember a leader telling me with ironic humor, "I always wanted to become president of the company, so all those people would serve *me*. I found out instead that I was there to serve *them*." That's the difference between **BEING** leader and **DOING** leader.

Peter Drucker pointed out that rising in organizational influence actually results in having less time of your own:

The executive's time tends to belong to everybody else. If one attempted to define an "executive" operationally ... one would have to define him as a captive of the organization.[2]

That description is a far cry from the illusions of power and autonomy many believe.

The higher you rise in an organization, the less you are called upon to *do* work so much as *seeing to it that the right work gets done*. That means you have to spend more and more time giving leadership ... sharing a vision ... clarifying focus and priorities ... promoting cultural values ... providing subordinates with guidance and resources to do their jobs ... following up, correcting, and coaching ... identifying opportunities and threats ... resolving snags in organizational processes ... on and on. Time demands on you multiply. You are truly serving the organization and its people.

Ultimately, the proof that you are successful as a leader is not what you do, but what *your team or organization accomplishes as a result of what you do*. Leadership requires a different definition of success than what is assumed by many excellent individual performers. Servant leadership is therefore not just some category or type of leadership. I argue that, looked at the right way, *all* effective leadership is servant leadership.

What servant leadership is *not*

Because of several common misconceptions, I'd like to first address what servant leadership is not.

Servant leadership is <u>not</u> doing anything anybody wants you to do.

I think this misconception is part of a larger one about what a "servant" is. There are widespread beliefs that if you are a good servant, or "have a servant's heart," you will do anything you are asked to do. That idea is absolutely false. I may have a servant's attitude, but I am still responsible to make good decisions about the use of my time and energies according to higher purposes and for a host of other reasons. I can, in other words, be a good servant and still say no to a request.

Servant leadership is <u>not</u> working below your ability and potential.

This confusion arises partly from admirable humility. Someone says, "I'm not 'too good' or 'above doing' some menial task because I don't think I'm better than other people." Good. However, as a valuable member of a team or organization, you are not fulfilling your role properly if you work on a regular basis beneath your ability and responsibility.

When Kate, a regional manager over more than a dozen medical offices, arrived for our coaching session, I couldn't help noticing that she looked especially tired. She explained, "I worked most of the last few days helping get a new office ready to open. We had to move refrigerators, boxes, and equipment, and I'm sore."

"Why were you moving those things yourself?" I asked.

"We did it ourselves to save the company money," she answered.

Kate was not expecting my next comment: "I didn't realize you were working for free."

We went on to discuss the reality of the situation. I asked her to calculate her salary by an hourly estimate (to herself), and pointed out, "You didn't save the company money. The company just paid you, let's say, $50 an hour to move boxes and refrigerators, plus what it paid your office manager and the other employees whatever they make per hour. You could have paid a handyman and movers near minimum wage to do the same work.

"Most important," I continued, "what were you not doing while you were doing manual labor? You were *not* leading, communicating, training, or mentoring your leaders — the things the company is actually paying you to do. That money you were trying to save turned out to be pretty expensive."

No, as a leader you must always consider the real cost and value of the time you invest. Activity is not accomplishment, and working below your capabilities is not servant leadership.

Servant leadership is <u>not</u> abdicating your leadership or authority.

This one hits the bulls-eye. Whatever "servant leadership" means, it does not mean you stop being the leader or boss. You remain the one in authority with responsibility for results and for the effectiveness of the entire team. You can be a servant leader and still command respect.

This point is a good time to introduce two essential concepts: **Efficiency** and **Effectiveness**. Here are my working definitions of each:

EFFICIENCY means "*doing things right*." Efficiency means doing things quicker, easier, and cheaper; the philosophy that says, "Don't work harder, work smarter."

EFFECTIVENESS means "*doing the right things*." Effectiveness means pursuing the highest and best use of my time and efforts according to the role I play, taking into account my knowledge, skills, and talents.

Along with your **Leadership EFFECT**, I refer to these as the "3 EFFs": Three areas of focus that must always be on the mind of an effective leader: Effect, Efficiency, and Effectiveness.

In application, everyone in an organization should be interested in efficiency; that is, doing their jobs quicker, easier, and cheaper. Efficiency should be taught and encouraged throughout the organization or team.

Leaders must be particularly concerned with effectiveness. Leaders cannot delegate effectiveness, neither their own nor the effectiveness of their team as a whole.

It is possible — and quite common in fact — to be highly efficient doing the wrong thing. You've likely heard the old saying that someone can be "penny-wise and dollar-foolish." Allow me to modify it for our current subject. You can be efficiency-wise and effectiveness-foolish. Peter Drucker said, "There is nothing more useless than doing efficiently that which should not be done at all." The higher you rise in organizational leadership, the more you must be concerned with *effectiveness*: "Doing the right things."

Let's consider a battleship. The Captain is surely interested in all aspects of the ship: the engine room, weapons systems, galley, infirmary, sanitation, and many more. But what if, instead of being on the bridge, the Captain spent inordinate amounts of time down in the engine room? Who will be guiding the ship? It might run headlong into an iceberg or reef. No, the place for the Captain is on the bridge. The Captain can delegate efficiency throughout the ship, but can never lose sight of his or her primary task: The safe and effective accomplishment of the ship's mission.

That's what it's like to be a servant leader: You can never fully delegate your responsibility for the well-being and effective accomplishment of your team's purpose.

What I learned from a wise mentor

When I was young in my professional career, I was significantly helped by Dr. Henry Brandt. Doc was one of most remarkable persons I've ever known, and he is probably more responsible for shaping my thinking and practices than any other man.

In his long career (he died in 2008 at the age of 92), Doc was a practicing psychologist, especially in the realms of family, marriage, and parenting; he wrote more than 20 books; and he traveled the world speaking and consulting with a variety of organizations. On top of all this, he also was a savvy businessman who started and led 6-8 business ventures on the side. Despite doing much of this simultaneously, he never appeared in a hurry.

When someone asked him, "How can you do all this?" he invariably answered, "By getting them done through other people."

Here's the difference between the average person and Henry Brandt. If an average person has a good idea, he or she thinks: "That's a good idea … but I don't have time for it. I'm too busy." When Doc had a good idea, he would think: "That's a good idea … *I wonder who I can get to help me do that?*" That made all the difference. It was his leading and managing abilities that enabled him to accomplish all that he did. Because of that pattern and practice, Dr. Henry Brandt was a significant and permanent influence in the lives of thousands of people and hundreds of organizations. I call that being effective.

Wrestling with the ideal of blending a servant's attitude with leadership effectiveness, I once asked him about it. He answered by referring to one of his earlier businesses — he had once owned a chain of ice cream shops that covered half the state of Michigan. Doc said:

"Let's say I walk into one of our restaurants and find the floor needs to be swept. I look over there and see the manager effectively busy. Over there the wait staff are effectively serving, and the busboys are busy working. I have no problem at that point picking up a broom and sweeping the floor.

"But I'm still the president. I'm the owner. I might be willing to pick up a broom in a pinch, but that doesn't make me the janitor. I would not be doing my job if I were running around to our stores and sweeping the floors.

"Serving has definition. I have a defined role with boundaries and purposes. I have a responsibility to remember my role, regardless of some momentary need."

Taking that illustration a bit further: Let's say the CEO of a company did pick up a broom and a dust pan. How would people react? I think if an average employee came around a corner to see their company's leader sweeping the floor, they might be understandably surprised.

But if that CEO is a genuine servant leader, the employee upon reflection would realize something else: *Yes, this is a bit unusual … but on another level it isn't. It's just an extension of what he does all the time: Whatever is required to serve the good of the company and its people.* Servant leadership is not something you turn on and off. It is who you are.

The mindset of servant leaders

Whether you lead a large organization or a small team, the mindset of a servant leader is basically the same. Here are seven characteristics of how servant leaders think.

1. Servant leaders serve something greater than themselves

Recall our earlier consideration of *Good to Great* where Jim Collins and his team determined that great companies are led by what they call Level 5 leaders. Collins doesn't emphasize the term, but he is describing servant leaders. They were all willing to subordinate their egos to the pursuit of organizational success.

Servant leaders are in pursuit of something greater than themselves. They are driven and almost obsessively-focused on a dream or a cause. It's not about them. It's about accomplishing some genuinely good work. For some, it's a vision of what their organization or team "could be" or driving toward ideals embodied in their mission, vision, and values. On the largest stage, it can be a fight to right great societal wrongs. On a small scale, it might be a manager deeply infected with an ideal of superior customer service. For servant leaders, the mission and vision are not just words, but unshakable motivating forces.

They multiply. People around them sense the genuineness of leaders like that and buy in to it. A movement begins as others progressively are converted to adopt the grand vision for themselves.

2. Servant leaders view the development and protection of a healthy culture as a top priority

A group's culture is the best predictor of future performance. Servant leaders know their group's culture cannot be left to chance, but deliberately build it according to defined values and philosophies.

They also know that healthy cultures are vulnerable and fragile and must be protected to endure. After all, every new person who joins an organization or team has the potential of diluting or changing the culture. Wise leaders select new members based on their suitability to the defined culture and make sure they are thoroughly indoctrinated in it.

3. Servant leaders know they cannot do it alone and view success as a team effort

Some conventional leaders like to be in the position of "a genius with a thousand helpers." Servant leaders do not possess that delusion. They know their human limitations and believe in the power of a diverse group of dedicated, talented people. Their focus is on how the *team* can function at its highest capacities, and they approach the selection, building, and maintenance of the team as their main occupation. Because of that focus, they are about *empowering* their people to develop and become as autonomous as possible.

Because of this, servant leaders work deliberately at **discouraging dependency**. There have been many foolish leaders who liked the ego stroking of "being indispensable," but that is a bad idea for several reasons. For one thing, dependency on you keeps your team from developing to their full potential. The achievement of the whole organization or team will be limited largely by what you personally are able to do, instead of what the entire group with its combined gifts and talents could accomplish.

Another reason why dependency is foolish is the jeopardy it puts the organization in. The question, "What if you get hit by a bus?" is a valid one. One of my closest friends was vice president of a large family-owned grocery store chain. For years, the company was led by Henry, one of the founding brothers. Whenever Henry was asked, "What is our master plan?" he would tap his temple and say with a smile, "Don't worry. I've got it all right here." Then one day without warning, Henry dropped dead. The company floundered for about four years before regaining its footing.

Servant leaders tend to be comfortably confident of their own strengths and aware of their limitations and weaknesses. Since their egos are not the main thing, they are also comfortable having other strong leaders around them. They don't mind sharing credit for successes and are not threatened when challenged, knowing that the organization is safer for having multiple people with the freedom and courage to speak up.

4. Servant leaders view themselves as being in the "people-development business"

Knowing that the success of the organization rests upon the quality and performance of the whole team, servant leaders devote significant time and effort to developing people and to channeling organizational resources to people-development processes and opportunities. John Schnatter, founder and chairman of Papa John's Pizza, exemplified this attitude when he said, "It's my job to build the people who are going to build the company."

This means the servant leader embraces the role of people-developer: Teacher, trainer, coach, and helper. This role is not hand-holding the unmotivated, but a people focus in concert with steady pressure to achieve higher levels of performance.

Having been involved in people- and leadership-development processes for several organizations, I can confidently say that without commitment *and participation* from the top, they fall flat. The top leader's attitude and commitment toward leadership development (or lack thereof) will flow down the ranks of the company. Servant leaders make that commitment.

5. Servant leaders ensure their people have what they need to perform

All large organizations are inefficient. Sometimes, success is determined by being less inefficient than your competitors. After years of coaching and training in many organizations, I still find myself boggled at the wasted time, inefficient systems, and ineffective activity I routinely observe. It is amazing that some organizations are as successful as they are.

An extremely important role of servant leaders is removing obstacles and hindrances, so people can do their jobs. They are also diligent to provide the resources, tools, and training people need to perform at their best.

One of the simplest things you can do for your people is to shorten, reduce, or eliminate meetings. Certainly, many meetings could be eliminated without harm. That's why they need to be examined periodically to see if they are still necessary. I believe in the philosophy, "When the horse is dead ... dismount." Some individuals may not need to attend a given meeting. Most meetings could be better and more efficiently led. And — addressing one of my major pet peeves — virtually all meetings could start and finish on time! It's really not that hard. You just need a chairman or facilitator who *intends to do so.*

Servant leaders know that many supposed "people problems" are really *system* problems, especially those that recur. Rather than displaying knee-jerk, "blame the person" reactions to things going wrong, they have the patience and diligence to find out why. They look behind problems to ferret out dysfunctional pockets of the organization and then fix those systems. They aren't concerned with discovering who's at fault so much as identifying and fixing root problems.

6. Servant leaders remember their role

Being the captain means in practice that servant leaders aren't trying to be everywhere doing everything. They remain "on the bridge" and allow other leaders and contributors to do their jobs. They aren't trying to be omni-competent geniuses or command-and-control puppeteers. Their role is more like the conductor of an orchestra: Guiding, teaching, and training a diverse group of musicians to play together.

Their sharpest focus is on personal and organizational effectiveness. They continually fight the battle of personal effectiveness, making sure they don't get down in the weeds and spend their time and energies doing lesser things. They also ask, "Are WE doing the right things?" They know they are ultimately responsible for the effectiveness of their leadership team and the organization as a whole.

7. Servant leaders are intentionally available to their people

After insufficient communication, the biggest complaint I hear in organizations is the difficulty people have getting their leader's attention. People need clear focus. They need to ask questions. They need the leader's sign-off to execute on projects. They need the leader's feedback on previous work. But they can't catch him or her. Their leader is a moving target. A FAST moving target. "I'm just really busy!" they explain. That's no excuse, but it does point to an important application: Leaders must be efficient managing *themselves* ("doing things right"), or they cannot be effective ("doing the right things").

As a servant to their people and organization, effective leaders realize that they must be **intentionally available** to their people and not leave it to chance or the slim possibility that some free time will appear. The best leaders I work with actually put time for their people on their calendars as well as taking regular "MBWA tours" ("Managing By Walking Around"). They intentionally schedule time for unscheduled conversations.

How do you find out what your people need from you? Simple. Ask them! Ask, "What do you need from me to do your job?" "What do you see me doing that someone at my level doesn't need to do, that you could take on?" "In what areas can you be given more freedom and authority to act?" If you periodically have conversations like that, you'll find your people to be ready with opinions and answers. You'll both be the better for it.

Leadership Development: Apply the *Karate Kid* principle

In the film *The Karate Kid*, a teenager named Daniel asks Mr. Miyagi to train him in karate, which the older man agrees to do on the condition that Daniel unquestioningly does whatever he says. In the next weeks, Daniel is required to wax numerous cars, paint a fence that looks a mile long, and sand what seems to be an acre of wooden deck. Finally Daniel blows up, exclaiming that he was supposed to be learning karate.

Mr. Miyagi begins throwing rapid kicks and punches at Daniel, each of which he instinctively blocks. Unknown to himself, throughout all those tasks Daniel has been training the muscles and reactions that will make him successful in karate.

That's the way leadership is learned. Not merely by being the best doer around, but by *learning the thinking and responses of servant leadership* until it becomes your DNA.

When you see a young person willing to step up and do what benefits the whole team ... acting with the big picture in mind ... willing to share knowledge and resources that help others succeed ... who shows signs of being a "true believer" in the mission, vision, and values ... who is generous in sharing credit with others ... and has that essential attitude for leadership, which is teachability ... take careful note. That's a leader on a growth trajectory and someone whose development you should cultivate.

Remember the *Karate Kid* principle. One of the secrets of leadership development is right here. The characteristics of a servant leader are some of the signs you are looking for to spot that elusive thing called "leadership potential."

Leading Insights

Part II: Proposition 7
The *Heart* of Leadership Is
Serving

- The proof you are a successful leader is not how much you do, but what your organization or team accomplishes because of what you do.

- You can never delegate effectiveness: Your responsibility for the well-being and accomplishment of your team's purpose.

- The mindset of a servant leader has these characteristics:
  1. Servant leaders serve something greater than themselves
  2. Servant leaders view the development and protection of a healthy culture as a top priority
  3. Servant leaders know they cannot do it alone and view success as a team effort.
  4. Servant leaders view themselves as being in the people-development business
  5. Servant leaders ensure their people have what they need to perform
  6. Servant leaders remember their role
  7. Servant leaders are intentionally available to their people

Leadership Proposition 8
The *Burden* of Leadership Is *Responsibility*

Victor Frankl was a Jewish psychiatrist and therapist imprisoned by the Nazis in the worst of the prison camps, including Auschwitz. He survived the Holocaust, and later wrote about his experiences and conclusions in *Man's Search for Meaning.*

In that book, he examines our fundamental need for significance and also our use of freedom. Everyone knows that one of America's proudest symbols is the Statue of Liberty, which stands on the East Coast. Frankl observes that liberty is only half the story and suggests that we should balance it by erecting a Statue of Responsibility on the West Coast.

On a more narrow scale, Frankl could have been talking about leadership.

We have seen that the heart of leadership is serving. Even so, it is true that the higher you rise in organizational leadership, the more freedom you receive; more freedom, that is, in the sense of more decision-making power over yourself and others.

That may sound appealing, and there is certainly an appealing aspect to being able to pursue your vision, chart your course, and make things happen. But that's only half the story. You also learn to an increasing measure Leadership Proposition 8: **The *Burden* of Leadership Is *Responsibility*.**

Leadership is not all about being in the spotlight and issuing directives. There is heavy weight on your shoulders, weight that you feel every day. To succeed in leadership over the long haul, you must choose to embrace the additional burdens of responsibility and learn how to bear up under them while maintaining yourself to function at your best.

You are no longer a private citizen

First-time managers run smack into this truth, usually to their surprise. Ellie was an excellent worker, the best "doer" in the office, whom most people considered a natural leader. When her own manager was promoted and transferred, Ellie expected to be selected to fill her place, which she was. A few months later, I was asked to work with her to help her progress in her new role.

Ellie came in quite upset for our second meeting, a mixture of anger and hurt. "I can't believe how the people in my office are reacting to me!" she exclaimed. "I used to be right in the middle of the social life of the team. Now I catch them clamming up when I come around and hear them whispering to each other. I had to get on Mike about coming in late, and he basically blew me off. I asked Millie to do a task for me, and she told me she didn't have time to do it! We all used to go to lunch together. Now they go off without inviting me to come along."

After listening and getting the picture, I said to her, "What you are running into, Ellie, is one of the truths of leading with authority that new managers often aren't prepared for. *You're not 'one of them' anymore.* The very fact that you are now the authority in the office puts you into an entirely different category.

"You are no longer just an employee, a free agent responsible only for yourself. You have to represent the interests of your company over your own personal preferences or the preferences of your team. People who used to be your peers and friends now look at you differently. Even if you continue to be a friendly, likeable person, your team members intuitively know that you have authority over them, that you can make them do things and hold them accountable for results."

For Ellie, this situation was a real struggle, and she wrestled with conflicted feelings. She had always enjoyed being "one of the guys." She really liked being in on everyone's lives, marital and parenting adventures, and sharing others' intimacies. Now she was clearly an outsider, and she didn't like this aspect of her new position: Discovering that being the leader puts emotional distance between you and others on your team.

Ellie was facing this situation for the first time on the front line level, but executives all the way up the ladder know this experience and the challenge of balancing personal and professional relationships with people over whom you have organizational power. It is very tricky.

Along with the change in relationships is this: The higher you rise in organizational leadership, the more you embody the organization to others. People no longer look at you as an individual. In some ways, you become a symbol, and in that sense, *less* of an individual person. The role is always with you, and the weight can be heavy.

This burden can be nearly a 24-hour-a-day role. As one community leader in my town said to me, "Anytime I'm in public, I feel like I'm walking around with 'DALLAS, TEXAS,' tattooed on my forehead. Anything I do or say may reflect on our entire city, positively or negatively. I'm not a person anymore."

I consider that attitude to be good advice for any leader. If you hold a position of leadership in your organization, work at thinking that way: Pretend you have the name of your organization tattooed on your forehead. Let that mindset remind you that anything you do or say will be taken as a statement about your entire organization.

You are responsible for effectiveness and results

We need to make sure there is no fuzziness or fog about this fact. Leaders are responsible to pursue effectiveness, their own and their teams', and ultimately are evaluated based on results. In the end, it won't matter how charismatic you are, how persuasive you are, or how well-liked you are. The question will be: Did you turn in the results?

As a leader, "results" refers to more than what you personally have done. The measure for a leader is what your *organization* or *team* has been able to accomplish. It will be a function of your professional competence plus every leadership principle we'll consider in this book.

You'll find that you have a different focus than the people on your team. Since you will be held responsible for the results wanted by those to whom you report, that fact will never be absent from your radar screen. Average team members who report to you usually won't share that viewpoint. They typically are concerned with how organizational decisions and directives affect them. You'll feel tugs and pulls from opposite directions and must learn to live with tension.

Special burdens on those with authority

If you are the head of an organization or a significant portion of it, the weight of responsibility will never leave you. Other members of your team may be free from thinking far into the future … free from considering potential threats on the horizon … free from worrying about the organization's cash holdings … free from worry about disasters … free from concern about a breakdown in IT hardware or software … free from worry about someone having an accident on the job … but not you! There is always something that can go wrong, and it can hang over you like a dark cloud. "Don't sweat the small stuff," some say, but leaders know better than to take that too far. "Small stuff" can blow up on you quickly.

There is also the principle of responsibility that comes from holding a position of authority in a hierarchy. Regardless of whether your structure is a traditional hierarchy or one of the currently-popular flattened organizations, you live with the fact that *you are responsible for everything that goes on in your sphere.* You are not necessarily at fault for the mistake of one of your subordinates, but you remain responsible because it happened on your watch. You are also responsible for dealing with the mess and for making it right. As the saying goes, "It may not be my fault, but it is now my problem."

Because you are a key decision-maker, you also live with pressure that comes from others. Peers may not be pleased with decisions or policies you make. Subordinates will likely be unhappy with many of your calls on issues. You might be severely criticized, even when doing the right thing. If you have a temperamental tendency to want to please others and make everybody happy, leading will be a challenge. If you give in to being a pleaser, you're sunk. If you resist it and try to make decisions based on principle, people will often be displeased. There's also the truth that you aren't always at liberty to tell everything you know or explain the "whys" behind your decisions. You will often be misunderstood and judged unfairly.

These examples are just some of the varieties of weight that rests on the shoulders of leaders in organizations, things the average person doesn't even think about. But if you are a leader, they are a daily reality.

Your influence can guide your team or throw them off course

Having been in leadership for many years, I still find it amazing how easy it is to forget how much leverage you have over your followers. I found I had to work deliberately at keeping that fact before me, lest I make decisions thoughtlessly that hurt others.

Even *good* leaders of organizations with positive cultures can easily forget how quickly-made, off-the-cuff decisions can cause ripples that grow in size as they cascade down the chain of command, causing major disruptions below. Impulsiveness in a leader is a hazard. Many a "simple" decision was easily made in a boardroom that caused a tsunami for the people who had to implement it. The Law of Unintended Consequences is always operating.

That principle is another reason to do some regular "Management by Walking Around" tours. A few conversations with people on the front lines will greatly enlighten you regarding some of those "simple and obvious" decisions you made in the executive suite.

I worked in my early years with John, a well-meaning, charismatic leader. He was energized by team conversations and enjoyed spontaneous, creative sessions. He would get stimulated and start issuing lightning-fast directives: "This is a great idea! Here's what we're going to do: Tim you do this. Jane, you do that. Will, get to work on this." We'd leave that meeting with an exciting new initiative for the month ahead.

The only problem was in the next week's meeting John would have moved on to something else. Someone would ask about last week's great idea, and he would say, "Oh, no, that's not what we want to do. What we need to concentrate on is …"

So there we were: We had taken that conversation seriously and put days of thought and effort into following what we were told to do … only to be informed later that we essentially wasted our time. After a few of those experiences you develop a skeptical wait-and-see attitude before committing to a new project. I vividly remember one staff member saying to me, "I never do anything John tells me to do unless he has told me on three separate occasions to do it. Then I'll know he won't forget about it." John's strengths were creativity and infectious enthusiasm, but you can see how that undisciplined creativity and enthusiasm can become a weakness.

Needless to say, our organization struggled mightily at times with initiative and accomplishment, much to John's frustration, but he was the real cause. He was not aware of how his impulsive decision-making and inconsistent focus hindered the progress of his team.

We actually were a pretty successful organization, even with those hiccups. How much more serious is impulsive and unfocused leadership when people's livelihoods are on the line!

Your decisions can seriously affect people's lives

Organizational leaders can develop a casual attitude toward their people and begin thinking of them as pawns rather than flesh and blood human beings. In a world where most people live paycheck-to-paycheck, employees and the families they support should be considered of utmost importance. Leaders and managers have the power to terminate their employees' ability to make a living there, even harm their careers and prospects for other jobs. It is morally unacceptable for leaders to take this responsibility lightly. Even more irresponsible is casually and capriciously cutting people when poor leadership and management are actually at fault for poor results.

As an executive coach working at all layers of companies, it is my observation that many firings have been at least 50% the responsibility of the *managers* involved. Too many times, they have failed to lead, failed to give clear expectations, failed to provide training and coaching, failed to give direct, honest feedback so employees knew exactly where they stood, and failed to hold employees accountable until those managers lost their temper and blew.

If you as a manager *have* done all those things properly and an employee proves unable to do the job they have been hired to do, fine, let them go. In such a case, the saying is true: "I didn't fire you. You fired yourself." That can clearly be the right thing to do at times. It's also important to recognize that there are automatic fireable offenses. I am not advocating softness regarding significant values, behavior, or performance. I am calling on those with organizational authority to recognize that with great power goes great responsibility.

In addition, there is also the responsibility of applying standards across the board impartially; that is, without respect to persons. Lewis V. Gerstner, Jr. says,

> Fairness or even-handedness is critical for successful leadership. Playing favorites, excusing some while others hang for the same offense, destroys the morale and respect of colleagues.[1]

It is my hope that anyone reading this book will be the kind of principled leader who recognizes the enormous responsibility you have to make sure people are treated fairly in the workplace, and are protected from unjust decisions of expediency.

You are not free to say whatever you think

One of the common misconceptions of rookie leaders is the belief, "Now that I'm the boss, I can say whatever I want." The truth is *exactly the opposite.* Communicating is too tricky and too impactful to be done thoughtlessly, *especially* for leaders.

If you are a person with influence or power over others, here are **seven reasons to carefully watch your words**.

1. Your words weigh more

People are prone to insecurity and anxiety, especially about their jobs. Employees continually have a finger in the wind, checking on the status and direction of their positions and companies, so in any typical organization, employees will discuss how things are going.

Imagine a couple of them in the break room talking when one goes off: "This place is falling apart! I think our company's going down, and we'll all lose our jobs!" Typically, the reality isn't that bad, and a coworker talks her off the ledge.

But imagine if the CEO of the company were to go off: "This place is falling apart! I think our company's going down, and we'll all lose our jobs!" What kind of impact do you think that would have? You know the answer. Panic and anxiety would surge through the whole company like an electric current — *even though in the two examples the words said were exactly the same.*

Why? Because the words of leaders "weigh more" than the words of others. This lesson is one of the most important for any aspiring leader to learn. You don't have the privilege of popping off with whatever crosses your mind. If you are a leader, you actually have *less* right to say what you think, because what you say creates waves.

That's not a bad thing. The weight of your words gives you one of the greatest powers of leadership, the ability to define reality. In fact, one of the worst things that can happen to aspiring leaders is to lose their influence, which usually happens because they have abused their verbal power. For a while, people will jump when the leader says to, but after a long series of verbal injuries, they will become numb. Once people have tuned out your communication as mere noise, you are done as a leader. So cultivate this power, and use it carefully.

From this master principle flow the following consequences.

2. Your suggestions become orders

You've probably seen it happen in a group or committee discussion. Several people go around the table giving tentative opinions, then the highest ranking person speaks. It may be that he or she simply intends to make a suggestion, but at that moment the conversation stops. Authority has spoken. The matter is decided. When you are a leader, your suggestions become orders.

If you're a discerning leader, being aware of this dynamic will lead you to become very careful and self-disciplined in group discussions. If you genuinely want to hear what people think and have a meaningful conversation, then you must fight the urge to give opinions prematurely because that's when people shut up and comply.

3. Your speculations become pronouncements

It's hazardous for leaders and managers to think out loud in the presence of others. While it's part of the responsibility for managers to consider the past, present, and projected future of an employee, talking in speculative terms about whether she or he "is going to make it" gets written in stone in others' minds. That impression becomes extremely hard for the most dedicated employee to change, no matter how diligent his performance.

It happens all the time in baseball. A young player gets labeled as a "utility player," someone without sufficient talent to earn a fulltime position, and he can't shake that label even if he bats over .300 for a full season. I've seen it often in business. An employee is labeled "not going to make it," and that label colors others' evaluations of her actual performance, regardless of reality. It's not fair to the person, and it costs the company much in terms of lost potential.

4. Your possibilities become promises

The parents among us have all learned this lesson the hard way. You said something like, "Maybe this Saturday, if I can get free, we can go to Chuck E. Cheese's." Saturday comes, and you have lots of things to do. The kids ask, "When are we going to Chuck E. Cheese's?"

"I'm sorry, I'm too busy today," you reply. If you have ever had small children, you know exactly what's coming next.

"But you promised!" No, you didn't promise, but you made the fundamental mistake of verbalizing a possibility — a highly desirable possibility to your children — and that possibility instantly became a promise in their minds. The words "maybe" and "if I can get free" did not register at all.

I've seen many organizational leaders make the same mistake (I'm sorry to say I've done it myself) in musing on possible promotions in an employee's future, something like: "You know, maybe one day after I'm gone, you'll be running this place ..." or "One of these days you'll probably be a supervisor ..."

Bad idea. Later it dawns on you that this employee you felt good about at the time is actually poorly suited for a leadership position. But now she or he has it in his mind that "someday" it's a given. You're in a tough position, especially when you must pick a better qualified person over them. You're seen as reneging on a promise.

5. Your doubts become fears

We have already considered this principle: Attitudes in a leader are extremely contagious and pass down the ranks quickly. Recall my saying: "A head cold in the captain becomes an epidemic in the crew."

It is simply human nature to have doubts, discouragements, and fears, but wise leaders learn they must keep them under wraps in the presence of others. What is simply a season of doubt in your mind will pass down the organization and become pessimism or outright fear in ranks. It's best to find a safe place outside the company to share those doubts and fears, and get the support you need to keep functioning with confident optimism.

6. Your criticisms become blows

Due to the weight of their words, leaders' compliments mean more and their criticisms sting more. Add to that the innate insecurities and sensitivities of people, and you have a mixture that gives leaders' negative words a cutting and painful edge. Keep this principle in mind: Compliment in public; criticize in private.

Yes, leaders and managers must point out and work at improving the negative, but the words you choose don't have to be hurtful. You don't have to say, "That was a stupid thing to do!" If you are in the habit of using the weight of your words wisely, a look in the eye and a simple "This could have been done better" can make an unforgettable impact. Sometimes less is more.

7. You have immense power to encourage or discourage

This final ramification is a summary of the previous six. Leaders have incredible powers of influence. Remember: There is never enough encouragement in the world. You have the ability to move and motivate people through this powerful force … or break them down through discouragement. What you say and how you say it will determine which it is.

This chapter addresses only some of the burdens leaders carry. Because of your impact as a leader, you must cultivate continuous self-awareness, always measuring the possible results of words and actions. You must consider when you are in public view *you are always on duty*. The ramifications of thoughtless impulsive actions and decisions are too great.

There is also the positive side: You can apply the leadership influence you have earned for good, to make things **BETTER**. It is possible to carry the weight of responsibility with joy and with the knowledge that you are doing something very significant.

Leading Insights

Part II: Proposition 8
The *Burden* of Leadership Is *Responsibility*

- If you accept a position of responsibility in an organization, you must give the organization your loyalty. You are not "one of them" anymore.

- Think, speak, and act as if you have the name of your organization tattooed on your forehead.

- As a leader with authority in an organization, you are responsible for everything that goes on in your sphere.

- Seemingly small decisions and actions can positively guide your team or throw them off course.

- It is morally unacceptable for organizational leaders to take their power over people's employment lightly.

- As a leader, your words "weigh" more than others', a power you can use for good or ill.

Leadership Proposition 9
The *Responsibility* of Leadership Is *Initiative*

During his coaching process, Kelly O'Connor shared with me a career-changing comment made by his CEO more than 25 years before. Daryl Flood, the founder of the company, had hired him to play an important role. Desiring to please, Kelly stayed close to him and sought directions on several occasions.

Finally one day Daryl turned and said firmly, "Kelly, I hired you because I believe you have the intelligence and ability to do this job. But I need you to operate at a higher level, and not wait on me to give you every directive." He paused. "Remember this," he added, "*The more you need me, the less I need you.*"

That last line provided a significant lights-on insight for Kelly, permanently shaping his attitude and habits for the career that followed. He realized the importance of taking **initiative** from his boss's perspective. When I worked with him years later, he was one of two Executive Vice Presidents for the company.

We saw in the last chapter that the burden of leadership is *responsibility*. We looked at many angles of the responsibilities (plural) that leaders confront. When you bundle them all together they come to a point, the particular responsibility that leaders cannot evade, which is my Leadership Proposition 9: **The *Responsibility* of Leadership Is *Initiative*.**

Responsible to act

According to the dictionary, *initiative* is "the action of taking the first step or move; responsibility for beginning or originating ... ability to think and act without being urged." From these phrases it is evident that initiative is about being a self-starter, about taking action on your own to make things **BETTER**.

Seen from the standpoint of attitude, the opposite of leadership is pessimism. From the standpoint of action, the opposite of leadership is *passivity*. Leaders are both *optimistic* and *active*. Leaders take time to think, which stimulates creativity, and embrace responsibility to take action.

Initiative is one of the characteristics common to all leaders, regardless of differences in temperament, personality, or style. They see an opportunity, a need, or a problem and take action to address it. Anytime someone sees a need and fills it ... whenever team members take action on their own without being told to do so ... when an employee walks into the manager's office having already thought through an issue and preparing recommendations ... they are showing initiative. In most cases, large or small, there have been other people who saw the same need but did nothing. They were not behaving like leaders.

Initiative is a leader's perpetual responsibility. Others may walk by a problem thinking, "Somebody should do something about this," but not you. You *are* the "Somebody." *You* are the one with the burden of *doing* something about it. From a leadership perspective, "doing something about it" does *not* necessarily mean fixing the problem yourself. The responsibility of a leader is to ensure that something is *done*.

In the early 1940s, England was being bombed on a nightly basis with devastating results. Churchill's practice was to take inspection rides through London and the countryside the next day to assess the damage. Afterward he would return to his office and write letters to the heads of the appropriate departments assigning them tasks. Churchill would close each letter with these words: "**Action this day.**"[1]

That's a leader taking initiative and insisting on initiative.

The value of a self-starter

General Eisenhower was especially appreciative of his assistant during the war. Stephen Ambrose writes:

His chief of staff, Gen. Walter B. Smith, had been with him since mid-1942. Eisenhower characterized Smith as "the perfect chief of staff," a crutch to a one-legged man. "I wish I had a dozen like him," Eisenhower told a friend. "If I did, I would simply buy a fishing rod and write home every week about my wonderful accomplishments in winning the war."[2]

I promise you: Any employee who makes his or her superior feel like that is going to be noticed and valued.

The following is my subjective feeling, I admit, but it seems to me that the quality of initiative in our culture has become rarer over my lifetime. That might be bad news for businesses and indicate further decline in customer service, but for a perceptive and ambitious aspiring leader this decline means opportunity. It is your chance to stand out in the crowd.

Applications of initiative

A leader's responsibility to take initiative applies to all the subjects we have previously examined. Leaders are responsible to take initiative to:

- Build and protect their **credibility** — their **Leadership Effect**
- Communicate the need to work toward a **better future**
- Maintain and communicate **optimism**
- **Define reality** in a variety of ways
- Build and protect a healthy, performance-based **culture**
- Project **authenticity**
- **Serve** their organization and people
- **Address problems** with the intention of solving or improving them

In this chapter, I want to address some categories of initiative that I believe are especially relevant to the subject of leadership, categories that I find are often neglected.

Take initiative to think

You are a leader if you know where you are going and can persuade others to go along with you. The first requirement is to be able to answer the question, "What do you want?"

Without taking *regular, specific time to think*, it is not possible to answer that question. It's rare to find someone who carves out thinking time. I find person after person in all kinds of industries who are going through their day simply reacting to what is going on around them. They are running as fast as they can on a hamster wheel with few results to show for it. Their jobs are out of control, and they will remain out of control unless they make time to think and build a plan.

Where will you lead people if you are unclear on where you are going? How can you communicate your goals and objectives clearly if you are unclear in your own mind? Communicating clearly is a challenging art. To do it well requires time to think, deliberate focus, and concentrated effort.

For the majority of people I work with, time to think must be *planned*. If they wait for an opportunity to just happen, they find it doesn't. Their days fill up with activities and urgencies. As a first step, I recommend putting thinking time on your calendar like any other appointment.

For those who will make time for thinking, there are a variety of options. Some take 30 minutes at the beginning or end of their work day. Some channel time demands in order to open up an hour block, which they tenaciously protect. Many find it helpful to go to a coffee shop or restaurant alone. I've often done this myself, finding a change of scenery and environment an aid to creative thinking. Others can wall off a Friday afternoon to do concentrated individual planning. For most it is an experimental process.

Whatever approach works for you, taking initiative to ensure you have adequate thinking time is a basic requirement for effective leadership.

Take initiative to pursue personal and professional growth

Organizations are full of people who are waiting for someone to take them by the hand. "Nobody is developing me," they complain.

I reply, "The only person on this planet who is responsible for you is you. Ideally, yes, leaders in your company *should* be interested in developing their employees, but most aren't. Those that are interested are extremely busy and have too many other things to think about. They may be willing and able to be resources and mentors, but don't wait around to 'be developed.' *Take ownership of your own development."*

How? There are countless ways. Some obvious ones are by reading good books and articles and attending seminars and training classes. Many larger organizations have abundant training opportunities. The key principle is to apply initiative: Make the pursuit of personal and professional growth your lifestyle, not an occasional activity.

Take initiative in self-management

Mediocre members of organizations only do what they are *made* to do. They come in on time only if they are punished for being late. They get work done on time only to avoid negative consequences. They do the bare minimum required to keep their positions.

One of the simplest ways to set yourself apart as a leader is by *defying the norm.* Take initiative to manage yourself. Do the right thing because it is right. Be punctual because you choose to be. Take action to address an obvious need on your own without being told to do so. Show professionalism in personal presentation; that is, through dress, demeanor, body language, speech, and mature behavior.

I like how the French statesman Clemenceau defined liberty: "Liberty is the right to discipline yourself so as not to be disciplined by others." In a world of rampant mediocrity, even a person of modest skills and gifts tends to stand out by exhibiting the quality of mature self-discipline. Leaders do it as a matter of course.

Take initiative to seek coaching

Since I am a certified executive coach, I naturally believe in the value of coaching. Your organization may offer internal coaching, or you could seek out an external coach. When considering a coach, I strongly recommend you choose one who has a defined coaching process, rather than one flying by the seat of his pants. The well-defined process is one of the things that drew me to gain a certification in Sherpa Executive Coaching. Ask questions about your prospective coach's process, methods, and results. The best coaches can answer those questions with ease.

There are, of course, many informal coaches and mentors you can seek out, and I suggest you do. Among the great benefits of learning from those ahead of you is that you don't have to reinvent the wheel or learn everything the hard way. Others have struggled, figured out tricks and insights, and have amassed a treasury of wisdom. Leaders like that are usually happy to share what they've learned with a sincere seeker. Approach them and ask if they can spare some time for you to ask questions about their career and experiences. If they agree to spend some time with you, ask questions and actively listen. You'll be much the richer for it.

Take initiative to cultivate relationships

"Relationships" covers a lot of ground, so let me break it down.

Build your superior's trust

A standard complaint by employees is, "My boss is micromanaging me!"

I ask, "Have you considered why your boss, or any boss for that matter, might micromanage?"

They think and say, "Maybe because she doesn't trust me? She's worried that I might not get the job done right or on time?"

Bingo! This phenomenon is called "managerial anxiety." In my experience, most leaders don't want to micromanage anyone. Superiors, remember, also report to someone and are responsible for results. Naturally they get nervous if they are feeling doubt. The solution therefore jumps right out at you. The more you build your superior's trust and reduce their anxiety, the more freedom they will likely grant you. Your manager will turn his or her attention to some other person who is making them nervous.

One of the simplest things you can do to increase your superior's confidence in you is proactively communicate. The average employee would rather avoid the boss and only gives an accounting of their responsibilities when the superior specifically asks. A simple way to separate yourself from the common herd is to take initiative to offer an accounting of your activities. Simply ask him or her for a few minutes of time. Walk in with a bullet-point list of what you're working on. Don't over explain. Simply share your bullet points while offering to answer questions or elaborate where desired. Ask if they have any questions or redirections they wish to make.

If you follow this simple advice, making sure you *deliver* on your agreements, you'll earn much more credibility and freedom to do your work as you see fit.

Build relationships across the organization

No matter how technical the work, business is about *people* working with *people*, leading *people* and getting the job done through *people*. That means healthy collaborative relationships are central to success in any organization.

I have found myself baffled and amazed at running into people in companies who don't seem to grasp this. They believe that because of their secure positions based on their knowledge and skills (professional competence), it doesn't matter whether or not they get along with others in the company.

That is more than a character flaw. It is strategically foolish. For myself, I *want* to have good relationships with others because treating people right is part of my value system. *But even if it were not,* I have enough sense to know that it's *smart*. I know that I'm not an island. I need the help of others frequently. It may not be today, this month, or even this year. But sooner or later, I may need to walk into someone's office and say, "I have a problem, and I wonder if you could help me?" At that moment, do you think it will matter what kind of relationship we have? Of course! People like to help people they like.

There are huge amounts of wasted time, wasted money, and general inefficiencies in organizations from the simple fact that people don't like each other. This is another of the negative consequences of an undefined or dysfunctional culture.

Individually, you can decide to be better than that. You can cultivate positive relationships with most people with deliberate effort. Even if Person A and Person B don't get along with each other, I've found I can usually make friends with both of them. That's one of the reasons I've been asked to serve as a mediator between people or as a facilitator for teams that need to collaborate. It's because I've made it a point to build positive relationships everywhere I can and earn their trust.

An old rule about making friends is, "To make a friend, BE a friend." The same thing really holds true in business. Look for opportunities to be helpful to others. Speak well of others and of the organization. Seek to cooperate on solving snags of mutual interest. Refuse to be dragged into other people's conflicts by focusing on principles and making things **BETTER**. You'll gain a reputation as someone who's good to work with and who's willing to help others.

This does *not* mean positive relationships only with "important" people. There are few things more sickening than the display of those who suck up to people above them, while treating people below them like dirt. Principled leaders demonstrate character and class by treating all people with friendliness and respect. Again, besides being a matter of values, it's smart, too. The assistance of those below you is often the most critical help you can get in a time of need.

Wise leaders also know that the good will of the gatekeepers is essential. By gatekeepers, I mean administrators or chief assistants to top executives. They not only guard the gates of access, they are typically experts at getting things done and thus make marvelous allies. They can also make or break your influence with the most significant leaders because their *opinions* of people are listened to very carefully by those they serve.

Develop subordinates

In some ways we have talked about this directly or indirectly throughout this book. I would like here to offer a couple of specific applications. You can cultivate relationships with subordinates by **avoiding the "Superstar Syndrome."** Here's an illustration from the world of baseball.

Ted Williams was one of the greatest baseball players ever. Nine years after his retirement in 1960, Williams surprised the baseball world by accepting the job of manager for the woeful Washington Senators. He managed them for four seasons, including a final one after they moved to Texas and became the Rangers.

The Senators/Rangers were ... how shall I put it? *Terrible* is a kind word. Game after game, Williams watched his team from the dugout, wondering how any professional ballplayers could be so inept. I once heard one of those players describe a day Williams was watching batting practice. Grinding his teeth over each weak grounder after popup after lazy fly ball, Williams finally couldn't take it anymore.

"!@#*%!" he blurted. "Somebody give me a #@* bat!" The 50-something manager went into the batting cage and took his stance.

Whack! Line drive.

Whack! Liner off the outfield wall.

Whack! Over the fence.

Whack! Another over the fence.

Williams threw down the bat violently. "*That's* how you do it!" and stomped off.

The players standing around the cage stared at each other silently. All were thinking the same thing: "But you're *Ted Williams!*"

If you are a leader at a significant level, you are assumed to be good at what you do. Especially from the standpoint of your strengths, you are above and beyond the average person. Keep in mind that we tend to judge others harshly when we view them through our strengths. You simply can't lead effectively if you become frustrated with less gifted people.

Jan, an Executive Director who had worked her way up, had this problem. She vented her frustration with her managers, who were having trouble juggling the many difficult aspects of their role. Frankly, I believed the expectations for the managers in that company were unrealistic and a set-up for failure, but Jan wouldn't hear of it. When I questioned her on that point, she snapped, "I can do it!" That's the Superstar Syndrome.

Leadership is about investing in people's potential for growth. The best leaders aren't trying to prove their superstar status. They stay focused on developing individuals and molding them into a team that proves greater than the sum of the parts.

Back up to where the people are

Working for an important government agency, Teresa was a dynamo with a growing national reputation. If you had asked her subordinates what they thought of their leader, most would use the word, "intimidating." "She's hard to get to know," they'd say. "She always seems distant." "She only cares about the work."

While they liked and admired Teresa, many found her a discouraging role model. "I could never do what she does," was a common belief. Perhaps even more telling: "It's impossible to satisfy her. Nothing but perfection is ever good enough."

Teresa was not a bad person. Quite the contrary, she cared about people and was very personable in social situations. It's just that those qualities were overpowered when she was on the job. Her work was her passion, and it left little time or energy for niceties. Because her standards were so high and speed so excessive, she left people in the dust. She also admitted to labeling people "underperformers" who couldn't keep up (which included just about everybody), and that she tended to make this judgment "too quickly."

While Teresa enjoyed socializing in its proper place, she felt that there was no time for relationships at work. "I believe it is 'work first, play later.' You eat your dinner, and only then have dessert," she said.

I asked Teresa a question: "What is the primary purpose of a car?"

"To take you from Point A to Point B," she replied immediately.

"Right," I said. "And what is the purpose of the oil in the engine?"

"To enable the engine to work right. To keep it from burning up."

"Right again. Now, suppose I applied your view of human relations to my car? What if I said: 'The primary purpose of a car is to get me from Point A to Point B. Oil isn't essential; it's like playtime after work, or dessert after dinner. So, I'm going to do my driving first and put oil in the engine later, after I get there.' What would happen to my car if I did that?"

"You would damage your engine," she said. "It might even burn up and stop."

"Yes, it would. So let me challenge your attitude toward the so-called soft skills. Time and attention for human relationships is not some add-on to work, and it is not dessert you enjoy only after the main course. Human relations are the oil that allows people to continue working at their highest levels by minimizing friction, discouragement, and burnout.

"I'm not talking about goofing off or wasting large amounts of time. The primary purpose at work is to work. But human beings have other needs, too, like a car needs oil and water. Things like appreciation, belonging, and caring *enable* us to work at our highest level."

Teresa thought for a moment. "So, what you're saying is, talking to people about ordinary things is not wasting time. It's like putting oil in the relation-ship to help them work better."

"Exactly. And besides that, if you never slow down, how and when are you going to develop anyone? When are you going to mentor people, share your knowledge, and help them progress?" Those points also got through, because Teresa really wanted to help people grow.

Teresa eventually came to understand the necessity of investing in the human side of managing. She worked at understanding what she was doing wrong and changed her behaviors. She took initiative to slow down to be a better leader.

Repair damaged relationships

No discussion of relationships would be complete without considering what to do when we make a mistake and offend or hurt someone. Those with too much pride will do nothing. Effective leaders know better. They have the humility and self-awareness to take initiative to do the right thing.

Apologize: Say, "I'm sorry."

Accept responsibility without excuse: "It was my fault."

Make sure there is **NO "BUT"** attached: "I'm sorry I cussed you out, BUT you did something to tick me off ..." An apology with a BUT attached is no apology at all.

Express your desire to do better in the future. Ask for help, if necessary.

The easiest thing to do is to try to look the other way, sweep it under your mental rug, or hope the other person forgets about it (they won't). Worse is to rationalize or deny your mistakes. Worse yet is to put the blame on someone else.

Mature people are comfortably aware of their own imperfections. They know they're not perfect and are not going to be perfect in the future. Accepting responsibility for a mistake does not hurt your credibility. Usually, it builds it. You will not hurt your reputation by admitting your faults, but you will surely do so by denying them.

Initiative means taking the first step, being a self-starter. While we cannot in this short chapter explore all the applications, I hope the importance of this quality is clear. To become a leader is to assume on your shoulders this particular responsibility of leadership.

Leading Insights

Part II: Proposition 9
The *Responsibility* of Leadership Is *Initiative*

- From the standpoint of action, the opposite of leadership is passivity.

- Initiative is a characteristic common to all leaders, regardless of differences in temperament, personality, or style.

- Adequate thinking time is a requirement for leading effectively.

- Take ownership of your own professional development.

- Take initiative to cultivate positive relationships with superiors, others across the organization, and subordinates.

- Avoid the Superstar Syndrome. Take initiative to develop your people and team.

- Effective leaders have the humility to apologize to others when necessary.

Leadership Proposition 10
The *Requirement* of Leadership Is *Courage*

A department director in his company, Steven was well-liked and knew the business. If he had a drawback, it was that he seemed almost "too nice" to be a strong leader. This trait caused some above him in the organization to wonder if he had sufficient strength of character and will to advance in leadership.

He functioned just fine under normal circumstances, but was hesitant to dial up and take charge when challenged. This became a particular problem in his weekly meeting with representatives of an outside client company his division served. As chairman, he was supposed to lead this meeting, but the others would come in aggressively, hijack the agenda, and put Steven and his team on the defensive. Everything was the fault of Steven's people, all the slip-ups were their failures, and all the responsibility for action was theirs.

Steven realized the importance of growing as a leader and improving his response to these situations. Dominating was not his default personality style, but he knew he had to change. Steven needed to find the courage to confront this challenge and prevail.

Every virtue at the point of testing

We have seen in the last two chapters, the burden of leadership is responsibility, and the responsibility of leadership is initiative. Those two principles lead us directly to this final leadership proposition: **The *Requirement* of Leadership Is *Courage*.**

In fact, this proposition touches every one of the nine previous ones. C. S. Lewis observed that courage is not simply one item on a list of virtues. Courage is every virtue at the point of testing. The application of every proposition when put into action requires courage on the part of a leader.

Winston Churchill made the same point:

Courage is the first of human qualities because it is the quality that guarantees all the others.

Without a measure of courage, no one would venture out to lead ... no one would challenge the present state for a better future ... no one would stand by their convictions ... no one would accept significant responsibility ... and so on for all the propositions.

What is courage?

We must first clear away some misconceptions. Some believe that courage is a feeling, but that is false. There is no feeling called courage that brave people possess.

The second misconception is that courage is the absence of fear. If you listen to people who have acted bravely in the face of terrible dangers, such as soldiers in battle or firefighters racing into a huge fire to save someone, they seldom say they felt no fear. In fact, many heroes have said, "I was scared to death the whole time." *But they acted nonetheless.*

No, courage is not the absence of fear. Courage is the willingness to do the right thing *in spite of* anxiety or fear. With this, many voices strongly concur. For example:

Courage is resistance to fear, mastery of fear — not absence of fear.
— Mark Twain

Courage is doing what you're afraid to do. There can be no courage unless you're scared.
— Eddie Rickenbacker (World War I fighter pilot)

Courage is being scared to death but saddling up anyway.
— John Wayne

We are not created equal in regard to inborn courage. Some are naturally bold, positively enjoying risky situations. They feel an adrenaline rush when attacking a scary thing. Most of us, however, aren't built that way. A degree of fear, timidity, or reluctance is normal.

We don't fear the same things. Some people enthusiastically embrace a physical challenge, but would break out in a trembling sweat if they were required to deliver a speech in front of a group. Others have no problem with public speaking to large crowds, but dread walking alone into a room full of strangers. Some strong leaders who are very effective at team leadership are afraid to hold direct confrontations with people one-on-one.

I often think of the apostle Peter in the gospel accounts. Most people know that the night on which Jesus was arrested, Peter denied that he knew him three times. Many have drawn the conclusion that Peter was a coward, but I vigorously deny it. That same evening when Jesus was arrested in the garden by a large armed mob, only one of the twelve disciples pulled out a sword and started swinging: Peter.

No, Peter was not a coward. But like most of us can potentially be, he was courageous in one type of situation, fearful in another. Peter had what I call "hot-blooded courage." As long as he faced a physical danger and a physical response was in order, Peter's your man. But in a "cold-blooded" situation, seated around a charcoal fire after midnight, he came up short. A little servant girl looked him in the eye and asked, "Aren't you one of them? One of Jesus' followers?" and Peter shrank back in paralyzing fear — the same Peter who was ready to take on an armed mob only hours earlier.

I believe this is an important observation. Many a leader has functioned successfully for years and grown quite confident. But life can deal you up something you never dreamed of. You can discover you are ill-equipped for this new challenge, and that you've been targeted right in a previously-unknown chink in your armor.

Many managers have developed a habit of "working up a mad" before confronting people problems. I think this is because their courage needs to be of the "hot-blooded" type. They use anger as a way to overcome their fear of confrontation (there are more effective ways to learn to do this). There are other kinds of courage, such as what Napoleon desired in his officers. He called it, "Two o-clock in the morning courage; I mean *unprepared* courage." It's one thing to be brave when you are preparing for an organized battle;

another thing to be roused without warning in the middle of the night and required to think clearly and act decisively.

The major application for you is this: Work at gaining greater self-awareness of both your strengths *and* weaknesses regarding courage because you cannot know what challenge waits around the corner. It may play to your strengths, but it may not. Knowing a situation might target your weaknesses can help you do what you would not otherwise do: Prepare and work deliberately at overcoming your reluctance in that type of situation.

Preparing for a test of courage

Back to Steven's story, we worked through his situation in depth. The first step was not to make a plan of action, but do the observation work necessary to understand what was happening. Steven looked back over the occasions when this chain of events occurred and began to identify common denominators.

First, Steven tended to approach those meetings as he did meetings in his own company. He was used to a positive, healthy environment of mutual respect and manners. That's the way he led his own team. But when he walked into a meeting with the other company's representatives, they didn't play by those rules, or by any rules Steven recognized. It felt to him like he'd landed on Bizarro World. Steven walked in relaxed rather than being on his guard, and got blind-sided. The result was confusion.

Second, since he was not in a vigilant frame of mind, he was not prepared with his facts and data. The attack came from unexpected directions, and Steven became hesitant and doubtful. That effect was aggravated by the fact that Steven tended to be a slower, systematic processor. Thinking quickly on his feet was not his strong suit.

Third, once these dynamics had begun, Steven felt a draining away of his self-confidence. He felt and acted defensively, rather than taking charge.

Having made these observations, Steven and I began working on possible actions he could take. After much discussion, Steven selected four keys from our conversation that resonated with him and that he believed were within his capabilities to apply. They formed an acronym that spelled "PACE."

P stood for **Prepare**. The root of his problem was walking into the meeting unprepared mentally, emotionally, and in regard to facts. He realized that careful preparation of *himself* and of the *facts and data* was the first thing he must do.

A stood for **Assume the leadership position**. That phrase communicated clearly to Steven the frame of mind and action he had to adopt. He was the leader of this meeting. He didn't need anyone's permission to function as one. Rather than passively responding to others' words and actions and looking for affirmation or permission to lead, he needed to assume that right and authority and proactively *act like it*.

C and **E** stood for **Confident Expectation**. Those two words communicated to Steven a clear *attitude* to maintain. Since he was doing what was necessary to think and act like a leader, he could also confidently expect others to follow his lead.

PACE worked beautifully. Steven walked into his next meeting with those people and took charge. He ran the meeting as a strong leader should and defined reality. He announced his plan to work through the agenda and began. He confidently answered the charges of the bullies, who became meeker and meeker as time passed. The meeting was conducted efficiently and effectively without significant trouble.

After hearing of the outcome, I stopped by a grocery store and bought Steven a jar of PACE® Picante sauce, which he kept on his office shelf as a humorous trophy of a victory won.

The lessons he learned did not end there, and Steven applied them in innumerable situations as he progressed. When I asked him on other occasions how a particular meeting or situation went, he would answer, "Great! I was fully PACED." Today he is the COO for a large company. He tells me years later that the picante sauce jar is still there by his computer, and he shares the principles with others who ask about it.

Steven's challenge did not involve great matters. No one's life was in danger. From such small wins, however, leaders are built. Those who have led in momentous times seldom arose out of nowhere. They, too, *learned* to lead step-by-step over years and learning to confront challenges with courage played an essential part of their training.

In what ways will your courage be tested as a leader?

You cannot predict how and from what direction a specific challenge to your courage will come, but knowing that challenges *will* come should move an aspiring leader to learn how to meet them. Each time you successfully face the hard thing before you, you bank more self-confidence and awareness that you are able to face the next one. Let me suggest some categories of testing you will likely encounter.

The inherent danger of leading

Previously in this book, I suggested that holding a position of leadership often means you come to embody the organization to your people. You'll find you become the focus of people's anxieties and fears. People intensely dislike anxiety, and they instinctively try to offload it to someone else. The handiest object on which to unload one's anxieties is the leader, the person who "is supposed to fix everything and make everything all right."

This tendency is not intelligent or rational, understand. If asked the question, people know that no leader can be expected to work miracles, magically fix everything, or control all reality, but that is exactly the point: They *aren't* thinking. They are *feeling*, and the history of the world is littered with leaders who were discarded because of unrealistic expectations and realities of which they were not at fault.

In extreme cases, think of the leaders in world history who were assassinated because they tried to bring about positive change and reform. Just from the 20th century you have Gandhi … Martin Luther King, Jr. … Anwar Sadat … Yitzhak Rabin … and many others.

Leading means rocking the boat, contending for a better future. For people who don't believe in it or don't want change, the easiest thing to do is to oppose or eliminate the leader. It can potentially happen in any sphere, large or small. If you hold authority, don't trust it to provide protection. People have an array of weapons and tactics to get rid of an authority figure.

Obviously, most leadership situations do not involve risking your life. But be assured: There is risk. It is far safer to sit back and be part of the crowd. It is far easier to try to do nothing to bring about change while criticizing those who do.

Leading means **being out in front**. This understanding is what Teddy Roosevelt meant when he offered this definition:

People ask the difference between a leader and a boss. The leader leads, and the boss drives.

You "drive" cattle. I'll wager, though, that you've never heard of a "sheep drive." That's why the traditional image of a leader is a shepherd. For example, if you see statues or paintings of the ancient pharaohs of Egypt, you'll often see them holding a shepherd's crook, symbolizing their (ideal) role as shepherd of the people. Shepherds provide for their sheep, protect them from danger, and guide them. Most of all, they are out in front leading. To be out in front opens you to a variety of hazards. Courage is required.

Receiving criticism

Sometimes it seems there is a law of resistance in leadership: For every action there is an equal and opposite criticism. Being criticized is simply part of daily life for people who try to make a difference in the world. It is irritating, but also true: Many times a leader is viciously criticized and resisted in the process of leading change, but sees that criticism melt away without any acknowledgement or credit from critics after the change works successfully. They just nonchalantly move on.

There are critics who call for *unrealistic answers*. Playwright and author John Galsworthy observed, "Idealism increases in direct proportion to one's distance from the problem." Answers are generally only "easy" from a distance and according to those who lack the imagination or will to explain how they could actually work in the real world.

There is the criticism of *second guessing*. Hindsight is 20/20. General Ulysses S. Grant said, reflecting on his war experiences:

> Later experience has taught me two lessons: first, that things are seen plainer after the events have occurred; second, that the most confident critics are generally those who know the least about the matter criticized.[1]

Any knucklehead can see that something didn't work after the fact. But leadership is done in real time without knowledge of the future. No leader is perfect, making every leader a potential target for critics, all those people who now confidently declare what he or she "should have done."

There are *deliberate* attacks from opponents or rivals. It is sometimes dangerous to engage with them because the very act of confronting them can harm your credibility more than the original charge. There's a folksy saying: "If you get into a fight with a pig, you both get dirty and the pig likes it." Courage and wisdom are sometimes shown through choosing not to fight.

You can face *criticism of your character*, which is especially painful if you are sincere. It is important to distinguish between accusations of *fact* versus accusations against your character.

I believe you should always answer a significant accusation of fact. If someone accuses you of embezzling from the company funds, you cannot allow that to go unchallenged. "Get out the books," you should say. "Call in the CFO. Bring in an independent auditor. Let's settle this right now."

But how could you reply to an accusation against your character? You can't open up a little door revealing your heart. No one can read your mind. There's no way to prove your sincerity or honest motives. All you can do is calmly assert that your intentions are honorable and offer to answer questions. Eventually, you must simply carry on. I find the following advice from Charles H. Spurgeon helpful:

If an enemy has said anything against your character, it will not always be worthwhile to answer him. Silence has both dignity and argument in it. . . . All the dirt that falls upon a good man will brush off when it is dry; but let him wait till it is dry, and not dirty his hands with wet mud.[2]

Some of the most painful criticisms come from your friends, people you have liked and enjoyed working with successfully over time. It hurts when people close to you misunderstand you or, worse, come to distrust you. Like other criticisms, there is often no way to prove your case except to calmly explain as well as you can and carry on, trusting future events to vindicate your judgment. Remember: "Truth is the daughter of time."

One of the hard parts about dealing with criticism is that you must, at the same time, *be eager and willing to hear it.* No leader is in more danger than a man or woman who has closed their ears to negative comments. Sometimes, listening to a negative truth is what will save you from disaster.

The ancient philosopher Augustine said, "As flattering friends corrupt, so quarrelsome enemies sometimes correct." Those opposed to us sometimes do us the favor of pointing out vulnerabilities. I tell all my coaching clients, "A criticism does not have to be literally true to be helpful." So listen through criticism to find if there is something valid to be aware of. Sometimes 90% of the criticism is baloney, but there is value in sifting through it to find the 10% that's helpful. The self-control and willingness to listen are signs of intellectual and emotional maturity, as well as courage.

Managing uncertainty

Many novices hold the notion that as you rise in leadership ability, all issues become clearer. No, often it's the opposite. The higher you rise in influence and authority, the fuzzier and more uncertain issues become. Andy Stanley put it this way (emphasis mine):

Contrary to what you might think, uncertainty actually *increases* with increased leadership responsibility. The more responsibility you assume as a leader, the more uncertainty you will be expected to manage. The cost of success as a leader is *greater uncertainty,* not less.[3]

A business plan is fine as a roadmap for how to get your organization or team from here to there. But no business plan is a substitute for the real-time wisdom and decision-making required in the adventure of life, where events are unpredictable.

A famous military maxim states, "No plan survives first contact with the enemy." In other words, once the shooting starts plans are out the window and soldiers must improvise. Eisenhower had this in mind when he said, "In preparing for battle, I have always found that plans are useless, but planning is indispensable."

No one knows the future, but the *process* of planning prepares you mentally to make effective decisions in real time. A clear head and courage are required to manage the uncertainty of real-life strategic decision-making.

A daily requirement

You need courage for:
- Attacking problems rather than ignoring them
- Maintaining your intellectual independence; i.e., thinking for yourself
- Addressing deviations from the cultural values and insisting on alignment
- Risking blame for failure
- Confronting poor performance or unacceptable behavior

Finally, you need courage to endure the *loneliness* that often goes with leadership.

Field Marshall William Slim fought with distinction in both world wars, and was later Governor-General of Australia. Invited to address the cadets at West Point, he remarked:

When things are bad . . . there will come a sudden pause when your men will stop and look at you. No one will speak. They will just look at you and ask for leadership. Their courage is ebbing; you must make it flow back, and it is not easy. You will never have felt more alone in your life.[4]

Leadership can indeed feel like that, in any sphere.

In the film *A League of Their Own*, Tom Hanks plays Jimmy Dugan, a burned-out former major leaguer assigned to manage a girls' baseball team. Near the climax of the story, one of his stars announces that she's leaving. When Dugan confronts her the player says, "It just got too hard."

Dugan leans in and says with low-volume intensity: "It's *supposed* to be hard! If it wasn't hard everyone would do it. The *hard* is what makes it *great!*"

The same is true of leadership. It can be challenging, scary, intimidating, demanding, and painful. But it can also be meaningful, stimulating, purposeful, enjoyable, and fulfilling. It's about making things **BETTER**, making a genuine difference in the world, having a positive influence in the lives of other people.

So I conclude my leadership propositions with this:

Leadership is hard. It's *supposed* to be hard. If it wasn't hard everyone would do it. But never forget: The *hard* is what makes leading *great!*

Leading Insights

Part II: Proposition 10
The *Requirement* of Leadership Is *Courage*

- Courage is every virtue at the point of testing.

- Courage is not the absence of fear. It is the willingness to do the right thing *in spite of* anxiety or fear.

- The process of leading exposes you to several tests of courage:
  1. The inherent dangers of leading
  2. Receiving criticism
  3. Managing uncertainty

- Always directly answer a significant accusation of fact. Don't let it go unchallenged. Present the evidence.

- If an accusation is lodged against your character, respond with silence or, at most, a calm rebuttal. Allow time and your track record of integrity and performance to be your defense.

- Your need to manage uncertainty rises with increased leadership influence and authority.

BETTER

The Fundamentals of Leadership

Part Three

Equipping for the

Journey

Part III: Introduction
Equipping for the Journey

Writing a book on leadership is like riding a tiger: Even if you are doing all right so far, how do you get off?

My aim in this book, as it is expressed in the subtitle, is to present the fundamentals of leadership: What you must *know* and *do* if you want others to follow you; truths important for anyone from the beginner to the advanced leader. This information I have tried to impart in Parts I and II.

There are dozens of applications to build on that foundation. Rather than make this a 500-page volume, however, I am going to bring it to a close after a few more chapters. I plan to continue exploring leadership applications in future books.

In this concluding section, the focus will be on some basic tools you can apply as you move ahead:

1. How to make an honest assessment of yourself according to the fundamentals we have examined
2. How to make the changes and improvements you want to make to be better prepared to lead
3. How to maintain yourself as a functioning leader and ensure that you have the structures and resources in place to sustain you over the long haul

From my website, www.StevensonCoaching.com, you can download a simple Leadership Self-Assessment I have developed for use with coaching and training clients. You can use this for current and future self-evaluations of your leadership performance. There are also assessments you can download from the same site to get feedback from others.

Leading is always an unpredictable journey, more like an epic adventure than a business plan or a step-by-step project. You don't know what you will face, but you are always better prepared when you begin by packing adequate equipment and learning skills to adapt to changing circumstances.

Chapter 1
A Look in the Mirror

A common misconception about executive coaching is that it is for those who are failing. While it's true that I am sometimes called in to work with someone on the brink, those are the minority of cases. The great majority of the men and women I work with are very good at what they do.

Executive coaching is about helping people who are already successful find ways to become even more effective. There is a reason the best golfers in the world continue to work with a teacher or coach. Differences at the highest levels are very small. For example, the difference between the No. 1 golfer on the PGA tour and the No. 100 golfer over the course of a year is an average of about *two strokes a round*. That doesn't seem like much, but it is very hard to make up even half a stroke per round at that level. It's also difficult to evaluate yourself and find where and how to make improvements. An objective coach is an essential help for those seeking the highest degrees of excellence in golf. It is the same for leaders.

Successful men and women typically know their strengths and have been maximizing their use for years. When you're talking about successful people, therefore, their most fertile areas for potential improvement will be found in addressing their *weaknesses*. That's also how champion golfers improve. They search for small aspects of their games where a stroke might be gained. They work strategically on specific skills such as hitting out of the rough or getting up and down from the sand. Their coach helps them zero in on where to target their efforts.

Executive coaching does much the same for leaders. We have examined throughout this book the critical importance of credibility in leadership. Unaddressed weaknesses can lessen or completely undermine an aspiring leader's credibility, and thus his or her Leadership Effect. The heart of coaching, then, is to help a client gain a higher level of **self-awareness** as the first step to improvement. If you are unaware of a personal failing, you are helpless. But if you become *aware* of an issue you can do something about it — assuming you want to.

Why *wouldn't* someone who is otherwise hard-working and dedicated want to improve as a leader? There are probably several reasons, but the most likely one is because of the cost attached.

The cost of improvement as a leader

The cost of improvement and success in leadership is *confronting the truth about yourself.* I mean truth in two ways:

1. The truth that's *within,* having the *intellectual honesty* to look at your thoughts, attitudes, desires, and values, and testing how harmonious they are when aligned with your words, actions, and ambitions.

2. The truth about yourself as *seen by others.* After all, a requirement of leadership is the ability to persuade others to go along with you. Other people will calculate your Credibility Bank Balance and be the ultimate judges of your Leadership Effect. Since you are not a mind-reader, you must be willing to listen to the opinions of others about yourself.

Does that sound scary? It is to most people.

Even some of the best leaders I've known have shied away from the truth, especially the second point. Rachel, for example, has developed and led one of the better companies I have witnessed. It is built on sound values and philosophies that are ethical, and effective. Rachel feels justifiably proud about the company she built, and she continues to lead her fellow leaders, insisting on integrity, serving attitudes, and excellent performance.

In later years, however, it became less and less acceptable to criticize Rachel herself. As a result, a small note of cynicism crept into her team. While she remained quite insistent about *their* development and performance, she subtly excused herself from some of the same scrutiny. Rachel was once dedicated and diligent about her own development, but not so much recently.

Her team noticed this change. Though it was seldom talked about openly, it could not fail to creep into their thinking, chipping away at their motivation and attitudes about work. Rachel may have been willing to avert her eyes from her negative quirks and inconsistencies, but nobody else missed them. If this process continues, that company's culture will decline, followed by higher turnover and less profit.

Realize: This is a *good* leader I'm talking about. It just illustrates how subtly and easily the reluctance to face the truth about oneself can occur. This battle is perpetual because it's simply part of human nature. And I'll confess: I had to fight against the same reluctance in my years leading organizations.

It shows again the importance of our final leadership proposition: **The Requirement of Leadership Is *Courage*.** In this case, it is the courage to hear and act on the truth as seen through the eyes of others.

A path for general self-examination

In this chapter, we will take a high-altitude approach to self-examination. You can dig into details later through downloading my Leadership Self-Assessment. To begin, let's return to the concept of your Leadership Effect.

Professional Competence
(Knowledge & Skills)

+   =   **Your Leadership Effect**

Personal Conduct
(Behaviors)

Your Leadership Effect will reflect the level of credibility you have in the eyes of potential followers. It is made up of **Professional Competence** (Knowledge & Skills) and **Personal Conduct** (Behaviors).

Competence must provide the platform

I was asked to coach Craig, the Director of Infrastructure for his company. He was over the technical means of work, such as phone services, email, networks, and equipment. Craig was a really good guy, likeable, and honest. Everyone liked him, it seemed, but Craig was fired before we made it half-way through his coaching process.

That's an unusual occurrence from my standpoint, so I went to his superiors to seek understanding. Unlike so many of my coaching clients, Craig's issues were not interpersonal or behavioral. It was all about his professional competence. Craig's performance showed a chronic lack of urgency, was checkered with mistakes, and his team proved inconsistent.

If there's anything you can do to tick off executives in a company, it's to allow their technical means of work to be unreliable.

As a coach, I cannot teach people the technical aspects of their jobs, those things found under the category of Professional Competence. Most people I work with are experts on specific subjects, while I remain a layman at best. Coaching addresses the category of Personal Conduct or behaviors. Even though I can't instruct them on the competence side, I always emphasize its critical importance.

Craig's story illustrates why *professional competence is the necessary prerequisite* for earning leadership credibility. His nice demeanor and likeable personality availed him nothing because he lacked that prerequisite.

How are you doing on the competence side of the equation? Here are some angles to consider. As a rule, is your performance in your area of responsibility ...

Quality work?
Timely?
Dependable?

Honest self-assessment is in order. If you see significant room for improvement from any of these angles, you already know part of what you must address.

Gather data from other sources. If your company or organization conducts surveys or assessments, those can be a gold mine of information. A limitation, though, is that the average person doesn't know *how* to draw insights from them. They are often multi-paged reports full of graphs, numerical ratings, and text, and the effect can be overwhelming.

It so happens that one of my gifts is sifting through reports like that and drawing helpful conclusions. You may need someone's help in doing so. One bit of advice: Unless there are major problems with your performance or behavior, try to identify no more than two or three observations where improvement would make a significant difference.

What kind of reviews have you received? If there is criticism about the quality or reliability of your performance? You must take that very seriously and dedicate yourself to showing clear improvement in those areas.

How would you gauge your superior in terms of managerial anxiety? Does he or she show confidence that you will do the job in a quality and timely manner? Or does he or she exhibit nervousness or insecurity about you? Your leader's attitude is an important thermometer of how you are perceived. Take it as your primary task to reduce anxiety and build their confidence in you. You can do that through proactively communicating and striving to produce dependable, timely, quality work.

Throughout this book, I have emphasized that professional competence is not enough to qualify you for leadership, but it is the necessary prerequisite. You cannot afford to let down in the performance of your responsibilities if you want to earn leadership credibility.

Getting other feedback

As I mentioned above, reviews and assessment reports can offer insights into areas of behavior you will want to address. Where else can you look?

Coworkers of all levels can be extremely helpful. You can ask for general observations about your or your team's work performance. One of my favorite methods to get helpful insights is the "one thing" question. Introduce it by saying something like this: "I'm working at improving, and so I wonder if you would help me. Would you fill in the blank in this sentence?" That

sentence is, **"One thing I can do to improve as a leader or manager is
_____."**

If others oblige you by filling in that blank, I have found that they
invariably share valuable insights and point toward areas where you can
improve. The key thing to remember is that *a criticism does not have to be literally
true to be helpful.* This activity is where you need to thoughtfully "listen
through" their comments. What are they really trying to say? Sometimes it's
obvious. Other times, it's not, but they are pointing to something valuable.

What would you learn if your superior answered, "By getting your work in
on time"? That should set off alarm bells and call for immediate and diligent
action.

What you would learn if a peer answered in either of these ways: "If you
would answer my phone calls or emails quicker." Or, "If you would be more
responsive when my team needs something." You would learn that you have
frustrated people by failing to be responsive.

What if the person you asked responded, "By being more positive in
leadership team meetings"? It may be you have developed the habit of being
negative or critical in speech.

If you manage others, ask your subordinates to suggest one way you can
improve as a leader or manager. What would you hear if they answered, "If
you spent more time with us"? Your first reaction might be, "That's ridiculous. We worked together for two hours yesterday." Regardless of how many
minutes you spend each week in their presence, they may be expressing a lack
of clarity regarding direction, priorities, or your expectations.

There is another line of questioning you can use. This one will bring out
how others perceive you in general.

Again, ask a few people if they will help you by filling in a blank (in this
case, ask for three responses from each person): **"According to your
experience, [your name] is all about _____."**

Let's say one responder's answers are "control," "discipline," and "reliability." A second coworker says, "punctuality," "professionalism," and "results."

From these two people you are hearing a lot about being self-controlled, focused, and businesslike. Those are good qualities, but notice: There are no words pointing toward relationships. How different an impression would you receive if they said, "enthusiasm," "friendliness," and "inspiring"? When you add people's responses together, look for commonalities, and do some reading between the lines regarding what they've said and not said. You can gain a great deal of valuable information about how others see you through this method.

There are some **rules for using these techniques**.

First, it is all right to ask for clarification or more information. You can ask, "What do you mean by 'more positive'?" or, "Would you please give me an example of what you're saying?"

Second, **never dispute their comments**. *Never* argue, deny, or defend yourself. Simply receive their opinion for honest reflection.

Third, **always thank them**. Anyone willing to put their necks out there and share an opinion is *doing you a favor*. Even if, after careful and honest thought, you decide their comment is invalid or unhelpful, that does not change the fact that they were willing to offer help.

Where an external observer is needed

Many of the applications we have discussed in this book are matters where you do some self-evaluation. There are other applications, however, where it is extremely difficult to evaluate yourself. In these, I suggest you seek a friendly coworker to observe you. Here are two.

Body language and other secondary communication

You communicate by much more than the words you say. Your posture, facial expressions, tone of voice, and gestures are giving your words their ultimate meaning to the listener. You are in fact communicating attitude, opinion, frame of mind, and intentions to a receiver, even when you say nothing at all.

While there are differing opinions on the exact percentage, all researchers agree that a large amount of communication between people comes through nonverbal means. Effective communication is inseparable from leadership, so if you aspire to be a leader you cannot ignore this subject. What you don't know *can* and *will* hinder you.

A serious approach to body language is not about "rules":
- Never cross your arms across your chest.
- Always look people in the eye.
- Never put your hands in your pockets.

The first thing I want a client to know is that body language is about *awareness*. It is about two questions.

First, *do you know what your body is doing?* It is amazing how many people don't. They are completely unaware that they are drumming their fingers … bobbing their leg … scowling when they talk to employees … raising their voice and intimidating others … nonverbally communicating boredom. As long as they remain unaware, they can't change anything.

Second, it means looking at yourself as a total package: *Are you communicating what you mean to?* The first step in communicating is *to know what it is you want to communicate.* The second step is *to make sure you are communicating exactly that.*

How do you *want* to be perceived? Do you want others to think of you as Professional? Competent? Reliable? Mature? Caring? If so, you cannot ignore the total message you are sending. How you sit, walk, stand, and appear are part of your "packaging."

Maybe most telling is how you handle interruptions and respond when you're caught unprepared. The role of leader means other people will need your attention. Interruptions are par for the course. Does your face say "You are bothering me, and I don't like it"? Does your body say "I can't wait for this to be over, so I can get back to my computer"? Or are your face and body saying "How can I help you?" When you're stopped in the hallway on the way to your office and asked a question, do you stop and turn fully to face the person with a relaxed posture and a friendly expression? Or do you remain physically turned away in the "ready, set, go" position, trying to get it over with as soon as possible?

You've probably heard the three real estate principles for determining the value of a piece of property: 1. Location; 2. Location; and 3. Location. Similarly, there are three principles for determining what you should or shouldn't do in terms of body language: 1. Context; 2. Context; and 3. Context.

Let's say you and I have had a long, casual, friendly conversation at a local coffee shop. At a certain point, I lean back in my chair, and fold my arms across my chest. What does it mean? Nothing … except that I need to shift my posture for comfort's sake after a long period of sitting.

On the other hand, what if you and I have been having a tense, unhappy discussion over a still-unresolved issue in an office, and I cross my arms across my chest and stare unsmilingly into your eyes. Would that mean anything? Definitely. In that context my body is saying *I don't like where this conversation is going.* Here's where sharpening awareness comes to your aid.

If you are walking to your office with something on your mind and you are interrupted by a subordinate needing help, you can restrain your natural impulse to physically communicate "I'm too busy for you." You can choose to turn fully, smile, and relax your posture, communicating "I'm here to help, and I'm interested in you" — *if* you are *aware.*

What if you're really tense inside and need to get to your desk? So what? No one can read your mind. All they can see is what's before them. You can communicate a spirit of helpfulness and interest, even if inside you really are in a hurry to get somewhere. If you do communicate that interest, you can quickly and tactfully make your escape without offending. People will accept it.

If you must hold an uncomfortable discussion with an employee about their performance, you will want to be aware of what your body is doing. You can choose to restrain any aggressive or threatening appearance and come across as professionally objective and yet caring.

Because of the difficulty of evaluating oneself regarding body language, it is usually necessary to get help. I suggest "deputizing" a friendly coworker to observe you. Ask that person to observe you in action and to give feedback. Ask them to observe your body language, facial expressions, tone of voice, and overall demeanor in public settings. You might be surprised.

Personal presentation

Personal presentation refers to the physical picture we bring to work: Clothing, hair style, grooming, and cleanliness. Women, of course, have traditionally had further complications to worry about in this area. Like body language, this subject is not normally about rules, but about context.

I remember when my father wore a suit to work each day, as did every other businessman in the city in a time when men usually also wore hats. Nowadays, it seems at least half of American businesses have relaxed dress expectations to casual wear, assuming there are expectations at all. And today there are a whole list of other considerations my dad's generation never dreamed of, like piercings, body art, creative hair styling and coloring, and more.

As with body language, there are two key questions: First, what do you want to communicate? Second, are you communicating that accurately?

When I joined a medical company in charge of leadership development, I had to consider this question. Most men in the company, I found, wore nice casual clothing: Long-sleeved button shirts with slacks. The IT staff tended to wear golf shirts. On Fridays jeans were acceptable. I could have dressed casually, but I reasoned: "They've hired me to be the 'leadership development coach.' Most people won't even know what that means until they see me in action. If I'm supposed to be the 'leadership development coach,' *I had better look the part.* I chose therefore to wear a jacket and tie to work every day, one of only a handful of men who did.

Clothing seems like a silly, trivial issue to many people today. They ask, "Isn't it superficial and bigoted to judge people's value on the basis of clothes?" Yes, it is, I answer. But like it or not, that's the kind of world we live in, and the kind of human nature you're going to encounter. You can rebel all you want about the way things "ought" to be, but reality is the way things actually are. I don't believe that "clothes make the man," but it is true that "the man makes the statement." If you want to be perceived as a leader, then your visual presentation will be the frame that accentuates or diminishes the effect of your performance and behavior.

I'm not an expert on fashion, hair, or the rest. I rely on others to help me, particularly my wife Suzanne. I certainly am no expert on women's fashion or hair, but other people are. My advice in this whole area of personal presentation is to find people who are knowledgeable and trustworthy and solicit their help.

Only you can determine what message you want to project, but others can help make sure you are projecting the image you intend.

Manners

There is only space for a brief mention of this extremely important subject. The concept of manners seems to have been lost in American society. What my parents took for granted and taught me about behavior in public no longer represents our culture's general assumptions.

Should it matter? Like the issue of clothing, the way things "ought" to be is irrelevant. Reality is what is. And the fact of the matter is that you will be judged by others according to the way you socially behave up against a whole set of unspoken standards. What good would it do to display professional competence if you are considered crude in conversation or labeled a barbarian because you don't know how to eat properly in a restaurant? Like the other categories we have considered, manners are about two questions: First, what do you want to communicate about yourself? Second, are you communicating that accurately?

I believe we live in a society that is progressively coarsening, but that does not determine my beliefs. I choose to be a gentleman, regardless, because that is a statement about me and my values. I do not intend to allow popular culture to dictate to me who I am or how I will behave. When I take my wife out, I open her car door and other doors for her. I pull out her chair and seat her at a dining table. I behave as a gentleman the way my parents and grandparents taught me, and Suzanne values being treated like a lady. Well-taught men of all social classes did these things a couple of generations ago.

Those behaviors are not even on people's radar screens now. Some businesswomen today are offended if a man holds a door and lets them go through first. Many professional women want to be treated exactly like a man, and I don't mean that as a compliment. To a great extent, the rules of proper behavior have become more unpredictable. What are we men to do? Here's my philosophy: I observe the persons I am with and seek to show respect. If I make a mistake, let it be on the side of good manners rather than bad. If I inadvertently offend someone, I can always apologize and try to accommodate their wishes.

As a man, I'm not really qualified to teach you women what it means to be a lady. From a male standpoint, it seems to me that being a lady has much to do with *expectations*: First, who are you and how are you willing to be treated? Second, what kind of behavior and conversation are acceptable in your presence? It's been my experience that men rise (or sink) to the level of behavior and conversation the women around them display and expect. I knew many ladies of previous generations that could halt any coarse language or behavior quickly with a withering look. Without a word their demeanor said, "How *dare* you say such a thing in my presence?" Strong men would melt away in shame. I urge you to take that power seriously. Decide what presence you wish to project, and do so. Don't let men determine how you present yourself.

I must say something about profanity. Back in the 1970s, George Carlin did a comedy routine called, "Seven Words You Can Never Say on Television." It was considered outrageous and scandalous at the time. He was arrested once for doing the bit during an appearance in Milwaukee. How things have changed. Now there are *no* words you can't hear on television, particularly on cable and other nontraditional outlets. Those words have infiltrated everyday speech in many a workplace, and to a great degree cussing has become normal and accepted.

My advice to you, if you want to build leadership credibility, is to defy the new normal and remove profanity from your speech. I'm not talking about being a prude or reacting like the Church Lady. In my younger days I was a fraternity man and a bartender, so there's nothing I haven't heard (or said myself, sad to say). I am convinced that using profanity reduces your leadership credibility, regardless of whether or not other people display a visible reaction. Choose to be a person of class who rises above the culture around you, and you will set yourself apart in a positive way.

Take this as an editorial comment, but I still believe in manners. Specific conventions of behavior may pass away, but people will always prefer to be around others who know how to speak and behave. You will do well in your leadership journey by learning and practicing good manners. At the very least, saying "please," "thank you," and "excuse me" should be automatic, everyday behaviors.

Much has changed, yes, but the heart of manners has not changed. Properly understood, it was never about "rules" alone. For decades Emily Post was a recognized expert on manners, and this is what she said:

> Manners are a sensitive awareness of the feelings of others. If you have that awareness, you have good manners, no matter what fork you use.

If you lack understanding or training on manners, that is easily remedied. Observe mature, classy people and learn from their example. There are also many good books that can teach you what you need to know. But don't miss the heart of what good manners have always been about: Treating others with respect, courtesy, and kindness. The "rules" come and go, but the heart of good behavior is unchanging.

You are being read by others

There's an old story passed down for more than 200 years. A Virginia man was standing by a river bank trying to figure out how to get across. Along came several men on horses, who proceeded to ride across the stream. The man watched the first and second riders go by, then he asked the third man for a ride. The third man agreed, and the Virginian rode across the river behind his host.

Afterward an excited person confronted him: "Do you know who that was? That was Thomas Jefferson! Why on earth did you ask *him* for a ride?"

The man replied, "I didn't know it was Thomas Jefferson. The first two men had faces that said 'No.' I asked Jefferson for a ride because he had a 'Yes' face."

There are people whose faces say, "Welcome." There are others whose faces say, "Beware of the dog!"

Are you aware of what *your* face says? What do you *want* it to say?

Leading Insights

Part III: Chapter 1
A Look in the Mirror

- The cost of improvement is confronting the truth about yourself, especially the truth as seen through the eyes of others.

- Professional competence is the necessary prerequisite for earning leadership credibility.

- Friendly objective coworkers can provide guidance in areas where it is difficult to evaluate yourself: Body language and personal presentation.

- Let your manners be determined by what you choose to be and do, not by the culture around you.

Chapter 2
Making Behavioral Changes

There were rumblings among the executives about one of their colleagues named Burt. Everyone acknowledged that he was eminently qualified in the area of software development and was an expert in developing and managing projects.

What was wrong? He was perceived by many as loud, obnoxious, and occasionally threatening. Others at the vice-president or director level were reluctant to work with him. The CEO expressed concerns about Burt's likelihood of succeeding there.

I found this feedback strange. I knew Burt well and thought highly of him. He was ethical, honest, and friendly. In fact, my experience with him indicated that he was as good-hearted as anyone I knew. His subordinates agreed. Burt's team members were uniformly happy to work under him, were highly-motivated, and liked him very much.

Like many of my executive coaching engagements, this one began by investigating and solving a mystery.

A process for changing behavior

As we saw in the last chapter, the first step for making improvements is to gain awareness. That requires the courage to hear the truth about ourselves as perceived by others. Often, that truth comes in the form of criticism, which may or may not be fair and accurate. The willingness to hear it and honestly weigh it is the necessary first step.

Whether awareness comes through self-assessment or the feedback of others, the big question remains to be answered: What do you DO about it? Even if you identify some fault, failing, or bad habit and you want to improve in that area, HOW do you go about it?

If you were to ask people at random, "Do you have any bad habits or traits you should change?" virtually everyone will answer that they do. They know they have faults and they know what they are. Why don't they fix them? There are several answers, but one of the most common is simply that they don't know how.

In the Sherpa Coaching method, we have a process for making behavioral changes. Since we use a lot of mountain climbing imagery as memory devices, it is called "Weakness Mountain." The process itself is simple to understand, though it can be a genuine challenge to apply. I will tell you, however, that it *works*. People who faithfully work this process are able to make significant and lasting behavioral changes. I do not mean to imply that they are always large changes. Sometimes they are small changes of behavior. Little things can, however, be leveraged to produce very large benefits.

The steps are 1. Acknowledge, 2. Observe, 3. Change, and 4. Evaluate. I will explain the steps briefly, illustrating with Burt's story.

1. Acknowledge

Acknowledge means to accept the validity of the weakness, fault, or bad habit. While it may be unclear at the beginning what exactly is going on, the key question is whether there is something significant here worth investigating. To the best of your ability, give it a name, which means identifying the problem in question.

Burt was turning off colleagues for some reason. He didn't yet know *what* he was doing, but whatever it was, he was offending and occasionally intimidating others. He wrote down, "Offending other people."

2. Observe

The Observe step is where I find much of the power of this simple process, and it requires extended explanation. One of the reasons people fall short in making changes they know they should make is they fail to do sufficient analysis to gain understanding. They tend to make a knee-jerk decision about what the problem is, and therefore attack symptoms rather than roots. It's like pulling the heads off weeds in your yard. The roots are left intact, and they grow right back.

As an example, many people name "procrastination" as one of their key weaknesses. How would you attack it? Merely "by trying not to procrastinate"? It doesn't work. Right off the top of my head, I can name several reasons *why* someone might procrastinate: Disorganization … desire to stay in their comfort zones … avoidance of boring tasks … fear of doing something unfamiliar … lack of courtesy toward others … inability to manage their work flow … perfectionism … poor prioritizing. Those are just for starters.

The main point is that until you identify *why* someone is procrastinating, you don't have any idea what to attack in order to improve it.

In the Observe phase you "get on the balcony" (a phrase I have adopted from Ronald Heifetz) to get a high-altitude look at the problem. You look for common denominators: When else has this happened? Are there common factors, such as certain individuals, time of day, or physical conditions? Are there triggers common to when the behavior is expressed?

Burt and I needed to discover what was going wrong in his interactions with peers. It was an important fact that his subordinates who worked around him every day did not share any of the negative opinions. They considered Burt a great leader. It also pointed to the fact that the more people got to know Burt, the better they liked him. The criticisms were all from people who didn't know him well or work with him often.

I had several opportunities to observe Burt in group settings. Along with conversations we had with the CEO and the VP to whom he reported, we put the pieces together.

There are some things about Burt I haven't yet shared. He is 6'8" tall. I don't how much he weighs, but the upper 200s would be a fair guess and not much of it is fat. He is just a large human being. Burt also has strong masculine features and a heavy beard. He could use a second shave around mid-afternoon. He also tends to have a loud voice, especially when he gets excited, which proved to be an important clue.

I noticed in a couple of leadership team meetings that Burt would occasionally get passionately involved in a discussion. I don't mean angry. I mean that he really *cared* about the work, and he really *believed* what he was saying. As he got excited, he would sit up straighter in his chair and begin to lean forward over the table. His eyes got wider and brighter, and his voice picked up in volume. He was not angry at anyone, but the result clearly looked intimidating. I made it a point to inquire whether this was happening in one-on-one meetings as well. It was. Burt's physical appearance, loudness, and passion were simply scaring people.

As we have seen before, this was another case of someone's strengths becoming a weakness. Burt's enthusiasm and passion for his work were major reasons why he was very good at what he did. His team who worked around him every day was used to him and had no problem with his personality or energy. In the case of others who didn't know him well, that passionate energy created an effect that was driving people away.

Good-hearted as he was, Burt felt badly learning this. He sincerely wanted to learn how to stop producing an intimidating effect on others, and we went to work. We had already noted some insights, but I wanted to peel the onion more to understand the source of this out-of-control passion. Why did it get stimulated, especially in those one-on-one conversations?

Burt's role in the company was to serve as a resource to other leaders and departments. He enthusiastically embraced that mission and only wanted to make work easier and more effective for others. As we talked, the problem became clear. In his passion to help, Burt mentally and emotionally *took ownership* of other people's projects. That was where he went wrong. As a servant to other leaders and departments, Burt was there to help *them* with *their* projects, *not to take them over.* In his passion to do his work, he forgot whose work it was. If the other person expressed disagreement, Burt would begin to debate with them, escalating the conversation further. Other executives felt overpowered and jittery as Burt displayed the physical symptoms of his energy.

These observations and insights provided us with the understanding to proceed to the third step of the process.

3. Change

After coming to understand a behavioral problem, the next step is to identify *a behavioral change within your control* to counteract it. The difficulty of carrying out the behavior change varies from issue to issue. Some actions are quite small while delivering big results. Others require serious mental concentration and willpower to apply change and break old habits.

The power of awareness is truly amazing. As the lights go on for a client like Burt, I have seen countless times that *awareness itself* is sufficient for significant changes to begin. By becoming aware of what he had previously been doing unconsciously, Burt began to intentionally slow down, lower his voice, and relax his body when he was around others outside his department.

I remember watching him during a leadership team meeting about that time. He sat back in his chair without tension, even slumping a little. When he spoke, it was noticeably more slow and measured. His efforts to do those things were obvious and a little amusing to me, but only the two of us knew what he was doing. The effect was that he appeared friendlier, more relaxed, and quieter. His ideas came across much better. I could see people paying more attention with positive interest.

As we worked on the issue, he identified his key applications. Burt began using the initials RSQ as his reminder (Relax, Slower, Quieter). He also was strongly impacted by realizing that he had been taking over other people's projects rather than approaching them as a servant offering help. He had a meeting on his schedule with a department head, and he worked with me to script how to talk about the project and communicate his attitude properly: "How can I help you with *your* project?"

Burt handled this and later opportunities successfully, and the negative rumblings went away. As other executives got to know him, they discovered what a good guy he really was, and what a great help he could be. His leadership credibility rose steadily.

4. Evaluate

The meaning of Evaluate is simple: Each time you make a change in behavior think of it as a small experiment. How did it work? Can you improve on it? If it did not work well, what else could you try? If it worked great, keep it up.

If the weakness in question is a serious, show-stopping fault, it must be your goal to eliminate its occurrence entirely.

In other cases, however, perfectionism is usually not helpful. Incremental improvement is good. Don't let an unrealistic, perfect ideal paralyze you from trying *something*. Another frequent saying of mine is:

It's easier to steer a moving car than a parked one. Get into action and try something, and improve on it as you go.

When you're working on awareness and trying to make changes, you are learning, and that can lead to further learning.

Further applications for making changes

After raising awareness enough to define the problem, the most important principle for improving weaknesses or faults is choosing actions within your control to counteract, interrupt, or avoid the offending ones. Simply "trying not to do them" doesn't work. Here are some additional points for making changes effectively.

1. Separate issues

Where there are two or more issues identified, *it is essential to separate them and attack them individually*. This process is the application of *discernment*. The word comes from a Latin root meaning "to separate or distinguish between."

Lion-tamers have traditionally used a whip and a chair as the tools of their trade. Even if that practice is now out-of-date, it is so well-known from decades of use that it has become a metaphor: "When I go in to lead that group, I'll need a whip and a chair." Have you ever wondered why? The whip is obvious, but why a chair?

Let's suppose the lion-tamer approached a big cat with a bare pole. A lion would simply swat that stick in half ... then, so much for the tamer! But when the tamer approaches the lion with a chair, what does it see? It sees *four legs coming at it*. Confused, not knowing which one to focus on, the lion hesitates. The lion-tamer then capitalizes on the lion's confusion to assert control.

Humans are the same. When we look at two or more problems at once, our thinking is confused and paralyzed. One common reason issues aren't solved is because people don't recognize that they are actually dealing with several problems at once, all jumbled together. It's like trying to organize a bowl of spaghetti. To be solved, issues need to be *identified, separated*, and *addressed individually*. That's discernment in action.

2. Formulate change behaviors positively

I learned this as a young father of five children (born within seven years!). Imagine what it was like taking five kids twelve and under to the grocery store. It was chaos. This one was doing cartwheels, these two were wrestling, that one was pulling items off the shelves, this one was dancing. You can easily find yourself constantly saying, "Put that back ... Quit the wrestling ... Stop running ... No gymnastics ..."

Negative commands don't work well. For example, if you say to a child, "Stop running," you are leaving them with all kinds of options. They think, "Can I hop?" "How about skipping?" "What about running backwards, does that count?" What would Burt have learned from a directive that said, "Don't scare people"?

What I learned early as a parent was *the power of positive commands*. I learned to say, "Walk slowly by my side." That is impossible to misunderstand. It can be disobeyed, but not misunderstood. Its positive formulation automatically takes in "Don't run ... Quit wrestling ... No dancing," etc. The same principle works for making changes in your leadership environment.

"Be early" is more powerful than "Don't be late."

"Speak well of the company and its people" is more powerful than "Don't be critical."

"Speak to others with courtesy and respect" is more powerful than "Don't use crude language."

Teaching leadership development classes to physicians, I have found this concept very helpful for improving their patient care scores. They are always in a hurry, often scheduled to have no more than 15-20 minutes to spend with a patient. They need to ask questions, diagnose needs, decide on prescriptions, and write notes on their laptops or tablets into the patient's electronic medical record — and at the same time connect personally with the patient and make him or her feel cared for. It would be a difficult challenge for anyone.

I'm not a doctor, but I could relate to their challenge because of my background in public speaking. My challenge after speaking was to connect with strangers in the midst of a large crowd and communicate interest in the individuals who came up to talk to me. Frequently, I only had 20-25 minutes at the most to take a break, get refreshed, and go back to speak again. I didn't want to come off as rude or uncaring, but I truly only had a few minutes. That's why I say it was similar to a physician's challenge.

Eventually I developed my own method. First, I adopted the philosophy, "Never *appear* in a hurry." The message I wanted to convey was, "I am interested in you." Now, I *was* in a hurry, but I didn't need to show it. Since no one can read your mind, you can choose to behave in such a way that you exhibit interest in others. Seeking to fulfill that mindset, these were my keys:

- Turn fully to the person(s)
- Smile
- Relax my body

After just a few minutes of behaving that way, I could make a graceful exit having made people feel I had connected with them. I could say, "I'm so glad to have met you. Thank you again for coming. Now I hope you'll excuse me, but I only have a few minutes before I need to go back and speak again." People would generally say, "Oh, of course! I understand." I could move on and no one was offended.

Physicians identify with that scenario. It helps them see that if they will spend just a few minutes connecting with people in an unhurried manner, they can proceed to make notes on their tablets and move on to the next person, having made that patient feel cared for. Any reasonable patient knows doctors don't have much time, but they want to be connected with as an individual. If they feel that connection, they will rate the doctor much higher, *even though the number of minutes are unchanged.*

I believe any busy executive or manager can apply the same technique and deal much more positively with the innumerable human interruptions that are part of a leader's job.

3. Use a memory device

Even when you sincerely want to make a positive change of behavior, it's easy to forget about it when life and work start revving up each day. When we act unconsciously, we tend to revert to old habits. So the question becomes, "What can I do to make sure I catch myself *before* acting in my old way?" Most of us need a trigger, some reminder or mental hook that keeps our goal before our eyes.

Burt shortened his reminder to the letters RSQ (Relax, Slower, Quieter). He wrote the initials on the corner of the white board in his office to help him remember. He also noted them in the corner of his calendar so he would see them before appointments. For Burt those reminders were sufficient to reign in his problem behaviors. Many of my clients pick acronyms that spell out their desired goals.

Mitch was an IT genius, a fact acknowledged by all who worked with him. He began, however, to get a reputation for frustrating people. He didn't care about their software problems, or so it seemed. I didn't get that impression talking with him. He seemed genuinely puzzled about why people were getting that impression.

After our investigation and analysis, we identified the problem. When someone came into Mitch's office seeking help and began to explain their problem, he went into problem-solving mode mentally. That's good in itself.

However, he *appeared* to zone out. While the person talked, Mitch stared into space, got a blank look on his face, and said nothing. "But I'm thinking about their problem!" he protested. "I'm trying to figure out how to solve it." To the other person, however, it looked like Mitch was blowing them off.

Mitch was unconsciously exhibiting an appearance exactly opposite to what he was really thinking and feeling. The solution meant making sure he gave the *right* impression.

After much discussion, Mitch identified his keys. They spelled **SYNC**.

1. **S** stood for **Smile**. It reminded Mitch to communicate friendliness.
2. **Y** stood for **Yes**. This represented Mitch's attitude: "If I can do anything to help you, the answer is yes."
3. **N** stood for **Nod**. Nod reminded Mitch not to appear to be zoning out; to be an *active* listener.
4. **C** stood for **Care**. This reminded Mitch to make sure he communicated verbally that he empathized with the person and was willing to help make things better as soon as possible.

SYNC worked wonderfully for him. Mitch pasted it to his computer as a reminder. I also periodically emailed him and asked, "Are you in SYNC today?" That unresponsive reputation evaporated fairly quickly as Mitch communicated the truth about his attitude and feelings.

Some of the most fun experiences I've had as an executive coach have been assisting people in creating ways to make positive changes and watching them succeed in their efforts. Many of their memory devices are quite creative and often hilarious.

- The executive with a small cartoon at her desk of a pig sitting on a fence by a farm
- The CFO who carried a small rubber ball with her into committee meetings
- The vice president who kept a *Matchbox* toy sports car on his desk.
- The executive director who had a cartoon cutout of Alfred E. Neuman (symbol of *MAD* magazine) on his bulletin board
- Steven, who created and applied PACE

Each of these meant something important to their creators, and each helped accomplish their goals. If the symbol or words represent something humorous or fun, that's even better. I tell all my clients, "Remember: No one but you needs to know what these symbols, letters, or words mean. As long as it works for you, that's all that matters."

I also share with them a famous military motto: "If it's stupid but works, it isn't stupid."

You CAN make behavioral changes and be a more effective leader if you want to and are willing to make the effort. The "Weakness Mountain" process of Acknowledge, Observe, Change, and Evaluate works for those who work the process.

Leading Insights

Part III: Chapter 2
Making Behavioral Changes

- The Weakness Mountain process is a tool for you to make significant and lasting changes in behavior.

- Perfectionism is generally not helpful. Incremental improvement is good. "It's easier to steer a moving car than a parked one."

- Where two or more issues are involved, it is essential to separate them and attack them individually.

- Positive directives are more powerful than negative ones.

- Use a memory device as a trigger for your behavior change: A word, symbol, object, or acronym.

- "If it's stupid but works, it isn't stupid."

Chapter 3
Self-Maintenance for High Performing Leaders

Reflecting on his experiences as a river boat captain, Mark Twain said, Two things seemed pretty apparent to me. One was, that in order to be a pilot a man had to learn more than any one man ought to be allowed to know; and the other was, that he must learn it all over again in a different way every twenty-four hours.[1]

To a captain piloting a boat down an unfamiliar river, the future is unforeseeable. Rivers don't flow according to connect-the-dots logic. They carve their own course through the countryside, and you never know what's ahead. It might be smooth sailing, or it might be a thrill-a-minute cascade down rapids and falls while you hold on for dear life and try not to capsize.

The unpredictable nature of leadership

Real-life leadership is also an unpredictable adventure, another reason why it is more art than science. Only rookies think leadership is about grand strategies and techniques systematically followed to assured results. Leading requires continual observation, diligence, creativity, and decisiveness to seize opportunities, avoid dangers, or respond to challenges. The day you think you've got it figured out and can expect a clear ride ahead is the day you turn a corner and see you're about to go off a cliff. The proud, complacent, self-sufficient leader can be humbled quickly.

This unpredictability requires you to be in the position of a captain on the bridge rather than getting lost in the details of various departments of the ship. *Leadership also requires you to be at your best virtually all the time*: Mentally sharp, alert, sound in judgment, resilient, resourceful, and reliable — *and* to have physical strength and energy sufficient to sustain you mentally and emotionally. If you're caught in a storm while your strength and alertness are subpar, the consequences can be serious for you *and* your team.

I'm not a prophet and do not claim to know the future, but I can predict this for you in your leadership journey: Trouble and challenges are ahead. If you function as a leader over time, you will experience the entire gamut of burdens and responsibilities we have explored in this book. It's not *if* they will come; it's *when* and *how*. That's just the nature and reality of this world.

Therefore, one of the final questions I want to pose to you as we near this book's conclusion is this: **How will you maintain yourself so you can be at your best** to meet the leadership challenges in your future?

The most effective and enduring leaders do not leave self-maintenance to chance. They apply a defined and deliberate self-maintenance system.

A 3-D look at your support system

In Sherpa Coaching, we use an exercise called "Support Mountain" to examine how well our clients are maintaining themselves. Sherpa Coaching has kindly granted me permission to reproduce it, and you'll find it on the following page. I do this exercise with every one of my coaching clients. For many, Support Mountain proved to be the most important thing we did. For some, this exercise has proven to be literally life-changing.

You'll see that Support Mountain is divided into three zones. Each of them is an angle from which to do the analysis, and each has a characteristic question that points the way. Working our way up the mountain, let's consider them in order.

1. INTRINSIC

For the first zone, called Intrinsic, the key question is, "**What?**" *What* things do you do for yourself that bring about recharging, refreshing, and relaxation? Think *activities*. For the time being, don't consider whether you've done any of them recently. Just put down what activities rejuvenate you, given the opportunity.

People commonly put down things like reading, listening to music, watching movies, exercising, playing sports, and doing arts and crafts.

Activities in the spiritual or faith categories fit into this zone as well. When we talk through it, I ask clients to be more specific about their answers to gain more understanding.

Sometimes people answer with activities I can't relate to. It doesn't matter. This is another application of that military motto: "If it's stupid but works, it isn't stupid." I tell clients, "If you tell me that flying on a trapeze relaxes and energizes you, my reply is 'Fly away!'" No one else has to understand or relate to what works for you. It's completely individual.

Put down as many answers as you can, creating more space, if necessary. Then we move on to zone number two.

2. EXTRINSIC

Extrinsic answers the question, "**Who?**" What *people* in your life can you go to for support, encouragement, advice, and, if necessary, accountability? Put down individual names here. These can be people with whom you share professional or personal relationships. Wherever the relationship exists, these are people you can count on for help when you need it.

They can also be relationships in a specialized sphere. Many people, for example, have a "best friend at work." When I worked for a medical company for five years, I built a great friendship with a man named Rodney. Early in my experience there, we discovered that we had much in common and became mutual supporters. I would often drop into his office or he into mine to discuss with complete confidentiality something on our minds. We helped each other through some challenging times. He and I seldom did anything together outside of work, but I considered Rodney a valuable member of my Support Mountain.

Clients doing this exercise put down spouses, parents, siblings, friends, mentors, peers, managers, and executives they know.

3. ENVIRONMENTAL

Finally, the top zone called Environmental answers the question, "**Where?**" What *places* can you go to that provide rest, refreshment, safety, and sanctuary? Like the Intrinsic zone, clients often come up with surprising answers. Once again, "If it's stupid but works …"

People have noted a room in their home, sometimes a specific chair, or a nearby park. Many have told me their car is a place of peace and recharging as they commute to and from work. Others have said they find a local mall a relaxing place to wander around. Clients sometimes cite a particular vacation spot. Of course, one drawback of a vacation spot is the infrequency with which you get to enjoy it, but still, it belongs on their Support Mountain.

I find this Environmental zone to be the one that surprises clients. Most haven't thought about places as being helpful to their functioning. Once considered, however, it makes sense.

What do you see?

After filling in Support Mountain, the first thing to do is to make general observations. Do some parts stand out? Is there balance or imbalance between the zones? Are there any glaring deficiencies?

A few experiences taking clients through this exercise are indelibly stamped in my memory.

Doris was the director of a large and important division of her company. An energetic and strong leader, she was all about service in both her professional and private life. As I walked her through Support Mountain, she quickly filled in the blanks in the second and third zones, even adding spaces for more answers.

When Doris finished writing, she stopped as motionless as stone, staring at the page. Quietly and slowly she said, "I don't do anything for me." Her Intrinsic zone ("What?") was completely blank. "I'm doing things for other people all day long at work and at home," she said. She was so thunderstruck by this realization that she did not resume conversation for several minutes. It led her to make some serious changes in her work and personal life.

In all the years I have been leading people through this exercise, I have had two individuals — a woman and a man — who were able easily to fill in the top and bottom zones, but for whom the Extrinsic zone ("Who?") was blank. In my mind I can still hear that woman's sad voice saying, "I don't have anyone in my life."

As in the entire coaching experience, the first step is awareness. Once becoming aware of a need, the key question is, "What do you want to do about it?" It also leads us to the second major question in the Support Mountain exercise.

How are you doing working your system?

I've had many clients who filled in the page with ease, adding spaces for additional answers. But completing the page really isn't the issue. I next ask, "How are you doing working your system?" Many of these same clients answer, "I haven't done anything on this page in six months." Obviously, it doesn't do you any good to know the answers if you're not doing anything about it.

In more positive cases, clients realize that they've neglected some part of it. "I've let physical exercise slip away," for example. Or, "I haven't gotten together with my best friend in months." Again, awareness allows them to take appropriate action.

Why *don't* people take seriously the importance of self-maintenance? The most common answer is **busyness**. Each morning they step into the rapid current of work and let their days "happen" to them, rather than building their schedules by design and planning time for self-maintenance. If you wait around for free time just to "appear" for self-maintenance activities, you'll be waiting a very long time. You either plan time for them, or you don't do them at all.

Obviously, most of us have limited time available for these things, and it's not reasonable to expect to do everything on our Support Mountain every week. But we *can* make time for *some* of them. As we have seen in other contexts, it's not about perfection; it's about raising your batting average.

Perhaps you can't get fit several hours of physical exercise in your schedule, but why not take a 20-30 minute walk during your lunch hour? What if you scheduled a lunch or coffee meeting with a friend once a week? Why not carve out a break in your morning and afternoon to give your mind a rest from work subjects? You'll get some refreshment, and your mind will be clearer when you return to your main occupation. The main point is to be determined and creative about maintaining yourself.

We must face another major reason people don't do things to maintain themselves: **They feel guilty about it**.

This problem must be attacked frontally. To care for yourself is not something to feel guilty about. First of all, it's a matter of self-respect. I ask my clients to write a specific sentence on the bottom of their Support Mountain page: "It is not selfish to see to my own well-being." A great many people *do* feel they are being selfish if they do something for themselves, especially those with a strong ethic of serving.

Second, investing in self-maintenance is simply facing reality: We are not angels or machines with unlimited strength, energy, and fuel. We run down, we wear out, we get tired, and we can get sick or injured. When we don't feed our bodies or get periodic rest, we begin to run on adrenaline. Adrenaline is made for short bursts of energy in a time of need, not for long-term functioning. People running on adrenaline are like someone revving up a sports car to high RPMs and holding it there while in neutral. Doing that would burn up your car's engine. We can do the same with our bodies. Then, as we start to wear down, we perform worse, our thinking and reasoning become foggy, and we are far more prone to mistakes. Despite some people's belief that they are working harder and accomplishing more, they are not. They would work far better and more effectively if they would take measures to refresh themselves.

To those who are all about serving others, I add, "Ok, I agree with you. Serving is a big part of my value system, too. But what good are you going to be serving others if you break down in the process? It's like saying, 'I know my car needs oil and water, but I need to drive to Houston (five hours from where I live). I'll put some in after I get there.' Good luck getting there.

"Besides that," I continue, "I know you've flown on a plane. When they make the announcement about oxygen masks, what do they tell people flying with children? *To put their own masks on first.* Why? Because if the adult passes out, who will be there to care for the child?"

I am dedicating some space here to make this point strongly because of the number of times I've dealt with it face-to-face with clients. It's amazing how many people resist the idea of maintaining themselves, and the servant-minded ones are the worst. So this is the bottom line for those with serving attitudes: *Care for yourself so you can be the best servant possible for others.*

Remember the nature of the world of work

At one of my previous organizations, I created and led a year-long training class for executives and managers on the basics of managing. While introducing them to the concepts of Support Mountain, I delivered a certain statement that never ceased to command people's attention. I have frequently been told that today, years later, it is the thing participants remember most vividly.

That attention-grabbing statement was this: "If you are willing to work yourself to death for the company ... the company is willing to *let* you."

In many companies, I would get into trouble saying such a thing, but to her credit, our CEO approved and agreed. She was a person of character who cared about the people who worked for her company. She did not want people abused and used up.

However, even if you work for a leader like that, *it remains your own responsibility to look after yourself.* No one else will take over that role.

In his valuable book, *The People Project*, Steve Laswell compares the world of business to the giant shark in *Jaws.* As they say in the film, sharks are genetically engineered to do only three things: They swim, they eat, and they make baby sharks. That's it. When the shark eats a person in the movie, it isn't being "evil." It's simply doing what sharks do.

Steve's point is that this is what businesses and organizations do. Their only purpose is to produce value, and they do this by consuming the time and energies of people. Steve suggests facetiously that businesses should post warning signs out front like the ones on the beach in *Jaws*. They should read, "WARNING: BUSINESS EATS PEOPLE!"[2]

Businesses (assuming ethical purposes, products, and practices) are not "evil" either. When they consume your time, energy, efforts, and contribution, they are simply doing what they do. That means you must embrace your personal responsibility to determine for yourself the extent of your investment. Only you can determine the extent to which your organization or company will consume your life.

My main advice is that you do it thoughtfully, deliberately, and with your eyes wide open regarding what it will cost you — because you can be sure: It *will* cost you, and in many ways.

Setting and maintaining boundaries

Without boundaries, we don't know where to draw the line. We don't know when to say no. We don't know when to stand up for ourselves. We aren't sure when and how to defend our authority. Texas Longhorns football coach Darrell Royal said, "A confused player can't be aggressive." That principle also applies in life and work. When we are confused about where the boundary lines are, we can become paralyzed in taking action.

Confidence comes from clarity, and that clarity can only exist when boundaries are identified and set *in advance*. What makes this subject trickier is the fact that there are different kinds of boundaries appropriate at different times and applications.

I organize boundaries into four categories. You will notice that these follow the outline of the three major questions we considered under the category of convictions, plus a fourth that arises for those in positions of authority.

1. Personal boundaries

Personal boundaries are foundational to all the others. They emerge from your overall view of human existence: What does it mean to be human? What is the meaning of life? What is your purpose for living? We Americans have this kind of thinking in our bones. Our founding document, The Declaration of Independence, says:

> We hold these truths to be self-evident, that all men are created equal, that they are endowed by their Creator with certain unalienable Rights, that among these are Life, Liberty and the pursuit of Happiness.

These convictions were a combination of Judeo-Christian belief and a philosophical assumption called Natural Law, the view that certain principles of truth and rightness are inherent in Nature and hold true everywhere and among all people.

The bottom line: *You are worthy of personal liberty and dignity simply because you are a human being.* You do not owe it to anyone to give up your individuality. No one has the right to be your master. You have the right, under your personal set of values, to live your own life and be treated as a responsible person worthy of respect so long as you do not harm others or break the laws of society.

A quick look at history proves that as a society we have often fallen short of this ideal, but that doesn't invalidate the ideal. Plus, knowing that the world around us often *does* fall short should remind us of the necessity to look out for ourselves and be prepared to defend our boundaries.

You require no other justification to insist on being treated with respect. This doesn't mean that you and I need to be touchy or have a chip on our shoulder, always looking for a fight. On the contrary, among the marks of being a well-adjusted and mature person are forgiveness, perspective, and patience with others. But when a mature person chooses to overlook an offense, it's a deliberate *choice* to do so, not because they don't have the right to stand up for themselves.

2. Principle boundaries

Principle boundaries deal with your moral and ethical convictions, and lead to your judgments of right and wrong.

Sometimes people talk as if right and wrong were something arbitrary, an optional choice like what color shirt to wear or how to cut your hair, but that's not true. Human societies throughout history have shown a remarkable consistency on the major principles. This view is proven by the universal human tendency to make excuses and offer justifications for our actions. If we didn't know within us what is right and wrong, we wouldn't be driven to explain "why the rules don't apply to me in this case."

This behavior is the realm of conscience. Each one of us has a private internal judge that alternately defends or accuses us about our choices. Psychologists will be among the first to tell you of the perilous emotional conflicts encountered by any person who continues to violate what they internally believe to be right.

Each one of us must take responsibility for ourselves in regard to ethics and morals. We have to work out in our own minds what we think is true and right in a given situation, and we owe it to ourselves to follow that judgment. It really doesn't matter if 55 other people are telling us that something is OK if we believe in our hearts that it's wrong. We need to stand firm and go by our best moral judgment.

This is not only important for individuals. A strong moral and ethical backbone in employees provides corporate protection for any organization when it is combined with the courage to tell the truth. Wise executives and managers *encourage* employees to speak up when they sense something is wrong. As I said previously, it's often the quiet voice of one person with a sensitive conscience that keeps a whole group from going wrong together.

3. Philosophical boundaries

Philosophical boundaries emerge from our judgments of *value and priority*. Unlike Principle Boundaries, these do not deal with "right and wrong." Philosophical boundaries are as individual as personalities, and vary widely from person to person. They are concerned with the investments of time, attention, and energy you are willing to give to various pursuits and to what degree.

When you know the answers for yourself, you have clear criteria for decision-making and boundaries. For example, if career advancement is your chief personal value, you might be willing to work an 80-hour week, whereas if you most value family balance, you won't (except perhaps in a time of dire need).

Understanding this dynamic is important for managers, too. Beating on a person whose chief value is family balance to maintain a 70-hour week is simply not going to work. Either the expectation needs to be adjusted, or the employee needs to move to another position without that expectation.

Of all the aspects of one's makeup, philosophical values may be the most changeable over time. For example, someone may not even consider health as a key value — until they get sick or injured. Then it shoots right to the top of the list. Life pressures can also push family balance or economic security to the forefront. Stage-of-life factors are important here, especially marital status or the age of your children. For example, there are professional ambitions you might happily pursue when your children are grown that you would turn down if they were under 10 years old.

Many conflicts in the workplace stem from unseen differences in values. We can observe other people's behavior, but we can't see the *reasons behind* the behavior, which can be traced back to values. Plus, because we naturally assume our own values to be the "right" ones, we tend to judge others harshly whose behavior or performance "doesn't measure up." That's why clarity on this subject is so helpful. By understanding clearly what our own values actually are, we can explain our choices and actions to others who differ. They may not agree, but at least they'll understand the reason for the differences.

The most important thing is not judging the priority values of others, but knowing your own. Flushing them out into the open helps people identify the reasons they are feeling conflicted and frustrated. When you've thought this through, you can set boundaries and make healthy and wise decisions.

4. Positional boundaries

Positional boundaries are based on *an authority role you play in relation to others:* a teacher in a classroom; a police officer on duty; a manager in an office. Many people become confused because they mix them up with personal boundaries, but they are not the same.

Let's say I have a neighbor who is a police officer. Joe is not a very likable person. In fact, he tends to be self-centered, rude, and inconsiderate. I don't particularly like his company, and neither do most of us on the street. In a dispute, I might even tell him, "You know, Joe, you're really a pain to deal with!"

He may disagree with something I'm doing, but I have no obligation to pay attention to him. To be blunt, in relation to issues of my personal life as a neighbor, I can tell him to buzz off.

But let's now say that I'm driving across our town one day, and I see a car with flashing lights behind me. I pull over, and a police officer walks up to my window. It's my neighbor Joe. How am I going to behave?

I'll tell you: I'm going to say, "Yes Sir." "No Sir." "Here's my license, Sir."

What happened to all my opinions about my neighbor Joe? They are exactly the same. But right at this moment, *Joe is a police officer on duty in uniform,* and I'm going to behave toward him with that in view. Because of this principle, they teach in the military, "Salute the uniform, not the man." I may not respect the man, but I must respect his authority.

This principle is the same for a manager in an office. Margaret may be a very nice and secure person who is unlikely to be touchy in answer to a personal affront, but what if she is disrespected or defied in her managerial role? Will she be "nice" and let it go unchallenged? *Not if she remembers her role.* She will take action to correct any disrespect to herself in her role as manager. Why? Because Margaret knows that being a "nice person" is beside the point. Allowing herself to be disrespected in her authority role as manager will undermine her ability to lead. I call this "flashing your badge." You hope that it's rarely necessary, but you should do so without apology when it is.

Stepping into a role of authority is not a small matter. We have already seen that you must face the truth that "you are not *one of them* anymore." Many new managers struggle with this, feeling new distance from former friends and peers, but it is simply a fact of organizational life. Yes, you can remain a "nice person" (I hope you do!), but that's a separate matter from *acting as the authority figure.* As such, you have a higher responsibility to the organization to represent and pursue its interests, just as a police officer in uniform has the duty of enforcing the law, regardless of how "nice" a person he or she is at home.

Therefore, if I am a leader with authority, I may be forced to confront behavior or performance that I might overlook as a "private citizen." It's not personal. It's being appropriately professional and demonstrating leadership.

Define yourself

The following is a predictable principle of life and leadership: **Define yourself or you will be defined by others**. With a single opportunity to pass through life in this world, I believe in defining myself. I urge you to embrace your God-given right to do the same.

Defining your boundaries in the four directions we have examined provides the structure and protection you need as you progress in your leadership journey.

Building and practicing your self-maintenance system provides the fuel and ongoing care you need to sustain you as you move ahead.

Leading Insights

Part III: Chapter 3
Self-Maintenance for High-Performing Leaders

- Leadership is an unpredictable journey with trouble and challenges ahead.

- The most effective and enduring leaders define and apply a self-maintenance system.

- You either plan time for self-maintenance activities, or you probably won't do them at all.

- Boundaries provide structure and protection in four areas:

  - **Personal** boundaries address "How I'm willing to be treated as a human being."

  - **Principle** boundaries address "What I'm willing to do ethically and morally."

  - **Philosophical** boundaries address "How I'm willing to invest my time and energy."

  - **Positional** boundaries address "How I'm willing to be treated based on the authority position I hold."

Epilogue
A Leader's Mindset

T he key to leadership is the leader. Throughout this book, therefore, the focus has been on you: Preparing you to lead by sharing what you must *know* and *do* if you want others to follow you. In future books, I will address specific applications for functioning as a leader, and we will plow through many of the "what-about" and "how-to" questions that have been stirred up by this study.

To bring this volume to a close, we should step back and consider some of the ordinary but essential facets of the way effective leaders think.

A single question changed my life

When I was fifteen years old, a man asked me a question that changed my attitude and went on to shape my leadership philosophy. It was a permanent attitude adjustment.

Mr. McDulin was the dean of youth sports in my hometown. He coached ten-year-olds through teenagers, mostly in basketball and baseball. I always wanted to play for one of his teams, but never got the chance. He knew me, though, and would offer encouragement when we crossed paths.

I loved playing sports when I was growing up, and particularly basketball. As a fifteen-year-old playing in a summer recreation league, I was as serious as serious could be about my game. I was scoring in double-figures regularly, hitting 14, then 16, and finally 18 points a couple of times. I was just burning to break the 20-point barrier and went into a game determined that this was the day. I did it. I was shooting well (and often) and finished with a new high of 23 points. "High" is the right word for another reason, too. I was glowing with pleasure walking off the court.

Passing through the doorway of the gym, I saw Mr. McDulin entering with his team. "Hey, Stevie," he said with a smile. "How'd you do?"

"I did great!" I answered. "I got twenty-three points!"

"No, no," Mr. McDulin replied evenly. "How'd *your team* do?"

"Oh. We lost," I said.

That was the question. Mr. McDulin didn't say anything else. He didn't have to. Before I took three more steps, I had received the message, and I have never forgotten it. From that day on, I never played a team sport again concentrating only on how I had done. Yes, I always wanted to perform well and gave it my best, but the success of my team became the main thing.

That lesson carried on to much more than sports. It's the attitude I have strived to maintain and spread through every organization I've been a part of.

Leadership is about the performance or achievement of the team, the organization, the company. This team approach is how effective leaders think, an essential attitude for leading. The day that you as a leader begin making it all about you, the slide to mediocrity or worse has begun.

How do you define success?

A persistent theme throughout this book is that individual production, no matter how excellent, is not enough to be a leader. How, then, is success determined? One person says, "I am a successful leader because of how much I do." Another says, "My success is not determined only by what I do, but by what is accomplished by my team as a result of what I do." The first person is thinking like an individual contributor. The second is thinking like a leader.

Excellent individual performance is not the same thing as effective leading and managing. Concentrating on your own contribution can actually get in the way of effective leadership. Many managers lose sight of their proper goal. They focus on "scoring 23 points," and forget that the real measure of success is a team victory. I run into this situation all the time as a coach, and I find it at all levels of organizations. These leaders are focused on being "the best doer" in the office. He or she is succeeding at that goal, but falling far short as an effective leader and manager.

Continuing the basketball analogy, these leaders are trying to be LeBron, the highest scorer on the team. Obviously, an organization is fortunate to have superstar performers, but that's not the same thing as leadership. Leaders think and act like point guards. Success is determined by how many *assists* they dish out rather than by how many points they score. A good point guard may score in single digits him- or herself, but they facilitate higher team scoring and victories through their court intelligence, passing, and leadership.

Excellent leaders measure their effectiveness by the quality, health, and performance of their team. This principle is why I believe that, properly understood, *all* effective leadership is servant leadership. As a leader you do whatever is required that is in the best interests of your team and its mission to facilitate the greatest cumulative results.

A leader's obligation

There is something leaders can do better than anyone, something that is the source of much of their power and influence: Give recognition, appreciation, and thanks to the people who enable them and the organization to be successful.

I have heard a common complaint in many of the companies I've worked with: "The only time my boss talks to me about my job performance is when I've messed up. He or she never tells me I'm doing a good job." The CEO of a company once told me directly, "If you work for me, about the only time you'll hear from me is if something is wrong." His behavior corresponded with that philosophy. The effects of this neglect are more serious than you may think.

I previously shared a comment by Max De Pree, but I cut it short. Adding the second sentence, he said, "The first responsibility of a leader is to define reality. *The last is to say thank you.*"[1]

We have considered a number of the reasons people care about their work, why they will expend their time and effort above and beyond the norm. Many of the **10 Leadership Propositions** touch on motivation. People follow because of their leader's credibility. They are made hopeful by optimism and a clear vision of a better future. They are stirred by the prospect of "being better than I am and doing more than I thought I could do." They are energized by daily immersion in a positive and healthy values-based culture.

Some would call those "leadership motivators," and I wouldn't disagree. There are also, however, many ordinary, everyday motivators that are just as important.

Everyday motivators

Seeking to answer to the question, "Why do people work at work?" surveys of front-line workers have provided the same answers for decades. People put their hearts into their work for reasons like these:

Belonging — Gaining a sense of identity through being an accepted part of a group; even better, being part of an effective team. For many people, going to work is the best part of their week because they get to spend time with their friends; sometimes, they think of them as family.

Recognition — Receiving praise for a job well done. Some people like public recognition, others prefer it shared one-on-one. As you get to know the individuals you lead, you can easily learn which it is for each person.

The best performers are usually highly motivated by recognition. If you neglect this need over a period of time, don't be surprised to see their performance fall off or witness their attitude turning sour. Great performers run on this high-octane fuel.

Appreciation and thanks — No one wants to be taken for granted or ignored. Thanking people for their contributions is a small, but powerful, form of recognition. It acknowledges their worth and recognizes their efforts. Besides, thanking people is simply good manners.

Relationship with a respected authority figure — People are motivated by up-close and personal contact with a leader they like and respect. This may be one of the least-known and least-appreciated of the motivators among leaders. Your personal attention, even in small doses, really matters to those who follow you.

I call these the **Basic Motivators**. Notice how simple they are, how little time or effort it takes to cultivate them. I strongly encourage you to make these practices such a ubiquitous part of your behavior that you don't have to think about it anymore. These should be ordinary, automatic qualities sprinkled throughout your interactions with people.

People do not work at work "because they get paid to do it." As a motivator, financial remuneration ranks farther down the list, usually around No. 6. Financial reward provides a necessary threshold up to a point for average employees, but then recedes in motivating power (though it ranks higher for executives).

Beware of demotivators

Motivating people does not take a lot. In fact, it's often what managers do to demotivate people that is the problem. Employees are typically demotivated by the leader:

- Ignoring them
- Failing to communicate clear expectations
- Communicating regularly negative or pessimistic messages
- Failing to provide recognition and thanks (perhaps most common)

Foolish leaders also diminish people's motivation by creating constant and unnecessary urgency, which usually is either manufactured or the result of incompetence. People have a finite amount of emotional energy. The higher they burn, the faster it drains away. After a while, you'll find a group in a high-stress environment becoming blasé and unresponsive to emotional appeals. If everything is an emergency, nothing is an emergency. What will you do if you really have an emergency? How can you ratchet up the sense of urgency for people who have been conditioned to view everything as urgent?

For these reasons, I firmly believe that an even keel and slow, steady pressure toward objectives is best for long-term effective performance. You'll find that people can sustain high commitment and sharp focus for long periods with a lower level of intensity.

Finally, if you really want to put a dagger in people's motivation and make it as bad as possible, simply do this: Accept all the credit for the achievements of a team. People don't miss it, and they don't forget it. This situation is unfortunately a common failing. Too many leaders have an ego problem that makes it painful to share the public spotlight with anyone else, even when recognition is richly warranted.

Your power to motivate

It doesn't take much to provide the normal, everyday energy that motivates people. You don't have to hire a brass band or shine a spotlight to give recognition. Saying "good job!" in public or offering a sincere thank you in private can do wonders. Picking up the phone to tell someone he or she did a great job can produce a lasting glow and fuel more achievement. A hand-written note of appreciation can make a major positive impact. You'll sometimes find that people save them and value them for years.

You do not lose by giving credit away. After all, you will always receive recognition for leading a well-running successful team. It's like being the quarterback in football: If the team wins, you'll be a star. Everybody knows who the quarterback is. Smart quarterbacks don't just soak up the accolades. They make sure to recognize and thank the others who seldom get their names in the papers, the big guys up front who do the blocking. Without those linemen sacrificing themselves for the good of the team, there would be many more bruises and far fewer touchdowns.

Wise executives do the same. If you have "president," "vice president," "director," or "manager" under your name, everyone knows it. If your organization or team produces superior results, you'll receive appropriate recognition for your leadership. By spreading around the credit for those results, you do not diminish your credibility or Leadership Effect. You enhance it. You are seen as a bigger person, and you earn more loyalty from your followers.

It's those people around you who are making you successful, not invisible elves. Acknowledge their good work, tell them you appreciate them, say thank you, and see how they do even more. It costs you so little, and gains you so much.

This is why principled, values-based, servant leadership is so powerful. It unleashes love, cooperation, collaboration, sacrifice, enthusiasm, effort, and all the intelligence and creativity of a group of people who are dedicated to a common cause.

This path is for leaders who want to make things **BETTER**.

May you richly succeed in pursuing your vision!

Stevenson Leadership Coaching

Leadership Development • Executive Coaching • Team Effectiveness

Tim Stevenson offers leaders and organizations expert guidance and coaching for effective leadership and leadership development. His home base is Dallas-Ft. Worth, Texas, but he frequently serves companies outside that area as well. He is also available for speaking engagements and workshops.

Contact information:

> **Phone**: 469-585-3982
>
> **Email**: tstevenson.csc@gmail.com
>
> **Website**: www.StevensonCoaching.com

Leading Insights

Since 2009, Tim has written *Leading Insights* articles on subjects touching leadership applications, managing tips & tools, and personal effectiveness. New articles are posted approximately twice a month. Past articles are archived and categorized on his website with free online and PDF versions available.

Anyone is welcome to download and share these articles. Many individuals have asked to have new articles emailed to them. If you would like to receive new articles when they are published, simply email Tim at the address above and ask to be added to the list.

Leadership Effect Self-Assessment Downloads

The Leadership Effect Self-Assessment mentioned in this book is available free of charge by visiting www.StevensonCoaching.com and downloading the PDF version. Available at the same location are versions that can be given to others to gain their input.

Notes

Part I

Chapter 1

1. Max De Pree, *Leadership is an Art* (New York: Bantam Dell, 1989), 134

Chapter 2

1. Jim Collins, *Good to Great* (New York: HarperCollins, 2001), 20

Chapter 3

1. Jim Collins, "And the Walls Came Tumbling Down," www.JimCollins.com

2. Daniel Goleman, "Leadership: Social Intelligence Is Essential," www.DanielGoleman.info, Feb. 28, 2008

Part II

Leadership Proposition 2

1. Jeremy Schaap, "We Will Catch Excellence," *Parade*, Feb. 3, 2008, 8

Leadership Proposition 3

1. Marcus Buckingham, *The One Thing You Need to Know* (New York: Free Press, 2005), 66

2. Stephen E. Ambrose, *D-Day* (New York: Simon & Schuster, 1994), 61

3. Ambrose, ibid.

Leadership Proposition 4

1. Eugene H. Peterson, *Run with the Horses* (Downers Grove, IL: InterVarsity Press, 1983), 163

2. Passed on by a friend several years ago. Source unknown.

3. Steve Laswell, *The People Project* (Next Level Executive Coaching, 2011), 133

4. Horace Porter, *Campaigning with Grant* (New York: The Century Company, 1897), 213

Leadership Proposition 5

1. De Pree, *Leadership is an Art*, 11

2. Scott Adams, *The Dilbert Principle* (New York: HarperCollins, 1996), 36

3. Adams, ibid., 37

4. *Success* (September 1995), 51

5. Louis V. Gerstner, Jr., *Who Says Elephants Can't Dance?* (New York: HarperCollins, 2002), 182

6. Terry Maxon, "Herb Kelleher's Jet Set," *Dallas Life Magazine* (Jan. 12, 1992), 8-9

Leadership Proposition 6

1. Henry B. Thayer, AT&T Archives

2. Frances Hesselbein, *Hesselbein on Leadership* (San Francisco: Jossey-Bass, 2002), 8

3. Ronald A. Heifetz, *Leadership Without Easy Answers* (Cambridge, MA: The Belknap Press of Harvard University Press, 1994), 268

4. Gerstner, *Who Says Elephants Can't Dance?* 219

Leadership Proposition 7

1. Matthew 20:25-28

2. Peter Drucker, *The Effective Executive* (New York: Harper & Row, 1985), 10

Leadership Proposition 8

1. Gerstner, *Who Says Elephants Can't Dance?* 239

Leadership Proposition 9

1. Stephen E. Ambrose, *To America* (New York: Simon & Schuster, 2002), 84.

2. Ambrose, D-Day, 69-70

Leadership Proposition 10

1. Ulysses S. Grant, *Memoirs of General U. S. Grant* (1885), Vol. I, Chapter XII

2. Charles H. Spurgeon, *Barbed Arrows* (Ann Arbor, MI: Baker Book House Company, 1980), 218, 219

3. Andy Stanley, *The Next Generation Leader* (Colorado Springs, CO: Multnomah Books, 2003), 68-69

4. Stephen W. Roskill, *The Art of Leadership* (1964), 152

Part III

Chapter 3

1. Samuel L. Clemens, *Life on the Mississippi* (1883), Chapter 8

2. Laswell, *The People Project*, 77

Epilogue

1. De Pree, *Leadership Is an Art*, 11

34284654R00141

Made in the USA
San Bernardino, CA
24 May 2016